GERMAN

T R A V E L M A T E

Compiled by Lexus
with Ingrid Schumacher

Chronicle Books • San Francisco

First published in the United States in 1991 by
Chronicle Books.

Printed in the United States of America.

Cover design: Kathy Warinner
Composition: TBH Typecast

ISBN: 0-87701-873-1

10 9 8 7 6 5 4 3 2 1

Chronicle Books
275 Fifth Street
San Francisco, California 94103

 printed on recycled paper

YOUR TRAVELMATE
gives you one single easy-to-use list of useful
words and phrases to help you communicate in
German.

Built into this list are:
– Travel Tips with facts and figures that provide
  valuable information
– German words you'll see on signs and notices
– typical replies to some of the things you might
  want to say.

There is a menu reader on pages 72–73, and
  numbers and the German alphabet are given
  on the last page.

Your TRAVELMATE also tells you how to
  pronounce German. Just read the
  pronunciations as though they were English
  and you will communicate – although you
  might not sound like a native speaker.

There are some special sounds:
oo is like oo in "soon"
œ is like oo in "book"
ō̄ is similar to the u sound in "huge"
ōw is like the ow in "cow"
k is like the ch in Scottish "loch"

If no pronunciation is given then the word itself
  can be spoken as though it were English. And
  sometimes only part of a word or phrase needs
  a pronunciation guide. Vowels given in italics
  show which part of a word to stress.

a, an ein; eine; ein [ine; ine-uh]
   10 marks a litre zehn Mark der Liter
   [tsayn . . .]
Abfahrt departures
aboard an Bord [bort]
about: about 15 ungefähr fünfzehn
   [oon-gheh-fair foonf-tsayn]
   at about 2 o'clock gegen zwei Uhr [gay-ghen
   tsvy oor]
above über [ober]
   above that darüber [da-rober]
abroad im Ausland [im ows-lannt]
absolutely! genau! [gheh-now]
accelerator das Gas
accept annehmen [an-nay-men]
accident der Unfall [oonfal]
   there's been an accident es ist ein Unfall
   passiert [. . . pas-*ee*-ert]
accommodation die Unterkunft [oonter-koonft]
   we need accommodation for three wir
   brauchen Zimmer für drei [veer brow-*k*en
   tsimmer foor dry]
» *TRAVEL TIP: as well as hotels there is the "Hotel*
   Garni" (bed and breakfast), "Pension"
   (boarding house), "Gasthof" (inn) or a room in
   a private house; look for the sign "Zimmer frei"
   or "Fremdenzimmer"; information on local
   accommodation available at railway station,
   look for "Zimmernachweis" or tourist
   information office
accountant ein Wirtschaftsprüfer
   [veert-shaffts-proofer]

accurate genau [gheh-nōw]
ache der Schmerz [shmairts]
  my back aches ich habe Rückenschmerzen
  [ish hah-buh rōocken-shmairtsen]
Achtung caution, danger; (spoken) look out!
  (announcement) attention please
across über [ōober]; **how do we get across?** wie
  kommen wir hinüber? [vee . . . veer . . .]
ADAC Allgemeiner Deutscher Automobil-Club
  equivalent of AAA
adapter der Zwischenstecker [tsvishen-sht–]
address die Adresse [ad-ressuh]
  will you give me your address? würden Sie
  mir Ihre Adresse geben? [vōorden zee meer
  eeruh ad-ress-uh gay-ben]
adhesive bandage ein (Heft)pflaster
  [–pflass-ter]
admission der Eintritt [ine–]
advance: in advance im voraus [im for-ōws]
  can we reserve in advance? können wir im
  voraus buchen? [kurrnen veer . . . boo-ken]
advertisement die Annonce [a-non-suh]
afraid: I'm afraid I don't know das weiß ich
  leider nicht [. . . vice ish ly-duh . . .]
  I'm afraid so ja, leider
  I'm afraid not leider nicht
after: after you nach Ihnen [nahk ee-nen]
  after 2 o'clock nach zwei Uhr
afternoon der Nachmittag [nahk-mi-tahg]
  in the afternoon nachmittags [–tahgs]
  this afternoon heute nachmittag
  [hoy-tuh . . .]
  good afternoon guten Tag! [goo-ten tahg]
aftershave das Rasierwasser [raz-eer-vasser]
again wieder [veeder]
against gegen [gay-ghen]
age das Alter [al-ter]
  under age minderjährig [minnder-yair-rik]
  it takes ages das dauert eine Ewigkeit
  [. . . dowert ine-uh ay-vik-kite]
agent der Vertreter [fair-tray-ter]

ago: a week ago vor einer Woche [for ine-uh vock-uh]

it wasn't long ago das ist noch nicht lange her [dass isst nok nisht lang-uh hair]

how long ago was that? wie lange ist das her? [vee . . .]

agree: I agree da stimme ich zu [. . . shtimmuh ish tsoo]

it doesn't agree with me das bekommt mir nicht [. . . buh-kommt meer nisht]

air die Luft [looft]

by air per Flugzeug [pair floog-tsoyg]

with air-conditioning mit Klimaanlage [. . . kleema-an-lahguh]

by airmail per Luftpost [. . . looft-posst]

airport der Flughafen [floog-hah-fen]

alarm der Alarm

alarm clock der Wecker [v–]

alcohol der Alkohol [–hohl]

is it alcoholic? ist das Alkohol?

alive lebendig [lay-ben-dik]

is he still alive? lebt er noch? [laybt air nok]

all: all the people alle Leute [al-uh loy-tuh]

all night/all day die ganze Nacht/den ganzen Tag [dee gants-uh nahkt/dayn gants-en tahg]

that's all wrong das ist ganz falsch

that's all das ist alles [. . . al-ess]

thank you – not at all danke – bitte [bittuh]

allergic: I'm allergic to . . . ich bin allergisch gegen . . . [. . . al-air-ghish gay-ghen]

allowed erlaubt [air-lowpt]

is it allowed? darf man das?

it's not allowed das ist verboten! [fair-boh-ten]; **allow me** gestatten Sie mir [gheh-shtat-ten zee meer]

almost fast [fasst]

alone allein [al-ine]

did you come here alone? sind Sie allein hier? [zinnt zee . . . heer]

leave me alone lassen Sie mich in Ruhe! [. . . zee mish in roo-uh]

Alps die Alpen
already schon [shohn]
also auch [ōw*k*]
alternator die Lichtmaschine
[l*i*sht-mash-ee-nuh]
although obwohl [ob-v*o*hl]
altogether insgesamt [inz-gheh-z*a*mmt]
always immer
a.m. vormittags [f*o*r-mi-tahgs]
ambassador der Botschafter [b*o*ht-shaffter]
ambulance der Krankenwagen
[kr*a*nken-vah-ghen]
    get an ambulance! rufen Sie einen
    Krankenwagen! [roo-fen zee ine-en . . .]
» *TRAVEL TIP: dial 110*
America Amerika [am-*ay*-ree-kah]
American amerikanisch *(person)* Amerikaner
(woman) Amerikanerin
among unter [*oo*nter]
amp das Ampere [am-pair]
and und [*oo*nt]
angry böse [burr-zuh]
    I'm very angry about it ich bin deswegen
    sehr verärgert [. . . d*e*ss-vay-ghen zair fair-
    *ai*r-ghert]
    please don't get angry seien Sie bitte nicht
    böse! [zy-en zee bittuh . . .]
animal das Tier [teer]
ankle der (Fuß)knöchel [f*oo*ss-kuh-nurr-shell]
Ankunft arrivals
Anlieger frei residents only
Anmeldung reception
anniversary: it's our wedding anniversary
heute ist unser Hochzeitstag [hoy-tuh isst
*oo*n-ser h*o*hk-tsites-tahg]
annoy: he's annoying me er belästigt mich [air
bell-est-i*k*t mish]
    it's very annoying das ist sehr ärgerlich
    [dass isst zair *ai*r-gherlish]
another: can we have another room? können
wir ein anderes Zimmer haben? [k*u*rrnen veer
ine an-dress tsimmer h*a*h-ben]

another beer, please noch ein Bier, bitte [no*k* ine beer bittuh]

answer die Antwort [*a*nt-vort]

what was his answer? was hat er darauf geantwortet? [vass hat air da-r*ō*wf gheh-*a*nt-vortet]

there was no answer *(tel)* es hat sich niemand gemeldet [. . . zish n*ee*-mannt gheh–]

antifreeze der Frostschutz [–sh*oo*ts]

any: have you got any bananas/butter? haben Sie Bananen/Butter? [h*a*h-ben zee ba-nah-nen/b*oo*-ter]

I haven't got any ich habe keins [ish h*a*h-buh kine-ts]

anybody (irgend) jemand [eer-ghent yay-mannt]

can anybody help? kann jemand helfen?

anything (irgend)etwas [eer-ghent et-vass]

I don't want anything ich möchte gar nichts [ish m*u*rrshtuh gahr nix]

apartment die Wohnung [voh-n*oo*ng]

aperitif ein Aperitif

apology ein Entschuldigung [ent-sh*oo*l-dee-g*oo*ng]

please accept my apologies bitte, verzeihen Sie mir [bittuh fair-tsy-en zee meer]

I want an apology ich warte auf eine Entschuldigung [. . . vartuh *ō*wf ine-uh . . .]

appendicitis eine Blinddarmentzündung [bl*i*nt-darm-ent-ts*ō*n-d*oo*ng]

appetite der Appetit [–t*ee*t]

I've lost my appetite ich habe keinen Appetit mehr [ish h*a*h-buh kine-en . . . mair]

apple ein Apfel

application form das Antragsformular [–trahgs–]

appointment ein Termin [tair-m*ee*n]

can I make an appointment? könnte ich einen Termin ausmachen? [k*u*rrntuh ish ine-en . . . *ō*ws-mah*k*en]

apricot eine Aprikose [app-ree-k*o*hzuh]

April April [appr*ee*l]

are sind [zinnt]
area die Gegend [gay-ghent]
  in the area in der Gegend
arm der Arm
around: is he around? ist er da? [. . . air . . .]
arrange: will you arrange it? können Sie das
  arrangieren? [kurrnen zee dass ar-ron-djee-ren]
  it's all arranged es ist alles arrangiert [ess
  isst al-less ar-ron-djeert]
arrest verhaften [fair-haff-ten]
  he's been arrested sie haben ihn verhaftet
  [zee hah-ben een . . .]
arrival die Ankunft [an-koonft]
arrive ankommen
  we only arrived yesterday wir sind erst
  gestern angekommen [veer zinnt airst
  ghess-tairn . . .]
art die Kunst [koonst]
  art gallery die Kunstgalerie
arthritis die Arthritis [ar-tree-tiss]
artificial künstlich [koonstlish]
artist der Künstler [koonstler]
as: as quickly as you can so schnell Sie
  können [zoh shnell zee kurrnen]
  as much as you can so viel Sie können
  [. . . feel . . .]
  do as I do machen Sie es mir nach [mahken
  zee ess meer nahk]
  as you like wie Sie wollen [vee zee vollen]
ashore an Land [an lannt]
ashtray ein Aschenbecher [ashen-beker]
ask fragen [frah-ghen]
  could you ask him to . . . ? würden Sie ihn
  bitten, ob er . . . ? [voorden zee een bit-en opp air]
  that's not what I asked for das hab'ich nicht
  bestellt [dass hahb ish nisht buh-shtellt]
asleep: he's still asleep er schläft noch [air
  shlayft nok]
asparagus der Spargel [shpargel]
aspirin eine Kopfschmerztablette
  [kopf-shmairts-tab-lettuh]

assistant der Assistent *(woman)* die Assistentin
asthma das Asthma [asst-mah]
at: at the airport am Flughafen
  at my hotel in meinem Hotel
  at one o'clock um ein Uhr [oom ine oor]
atmosphere die Atmosphäre [−fay-ruh]
attitude die Einstellung [ine-shtell-oong]
attractive attraktiv [−teef]
  I think you're very attractive ich finde Sie
  sehr attraktiv [ish fin-duh zee zair . . .]
Aufzug elevator
August August [ōw-goost]
aunt: my aunt meine Tante [mine-uh tantuh]
Ausfahrt exit offramp
Ausgang exit
Auskunft information
außer Betrieb out of order
Australia Australien [ōws-trah-lee-un]
Australian australisch [ōws-trah-lish]
  (person) Australier [−leer]
  (woman) Australierin
Austria Österreich [urr-ster-rysh]
Austrian österreichisch [−ish]; *(person)*
  Österreicher; *(woman)* Österreicherin
Ausverkauf sale
ausverkauft sold out
authorities die Behörden [buh-hurr-den]
automatic *(car)* der Automatik [ōw-toh-mah-tik]
autumn der Herbst [hairbst]
  in the autumn im Herbst
away: is it far away from here? ist es weit von
  hier? [iss ess vite fon heer]
  go away! geh (weg)! [gay vek]
awful schrecklich [−lish]
axle die Achse [ak-suh]
baby ein Baby
  we'd like a baby-sitter wir brauchen einen
  baby−sitter [veer brōwken ine-en . . .]
back: I've got a bad back ich habe
  Schwierigkeiten mit meinem Rücken [ish
  hah-buh shvee-rik-kite-en mit mine-em rocken]

I'll be back soon ich bin bald wieder da [ish bin balt veeder dah]

is he back? ist er wieder da?

can I have my money back? kann ich mein Geld wiederhaben? [kan ish mine gellt veeder-hah-ben]

come back kommen Sie zurück! [. . . zee tsoo-rōōck]

I go back tomorrow ich fahre morgen zurück [ish fah-ruh mor-ghen . . .]

at the back hinten

bacon der Speck [shpeck]

bacon and eggs Eier mit Speck [eye-er . . .]

bad schlecht [shlekt]; **not bad** nicht schlecht

too bad Pech! [pek]

the milk/meat is bad die Milch ist sauer/das Fleisch ist schlecht [dee milsch isst zōw-er/dass flysh isst shlesht]

Bad bathroom

Baden verboten no bathing

baggage das Gepäck [gheh-peck]

Bahnsteig platform

Bahnübergang grade crossing

bakery der Bäcker [becker]

balcony der Balkon

a room with a balcony ein Zimmer mit Balkon [ine tsimmer . . .]

ball der Ball [bal]

ballpoint pen ein Kugelschreiber [koogel-shryber]

banana eine Banane [bananuh]

band *(music)* die Band [bannt] *(dance)* das Orchester [orkester]

bandage die Binde [bin-duh]

could you change the bandage? könnten Sie den Verband wechseln? [kurrnten zee dayn fair-bannt vek-seln]

bank die Bank

» *TRAVEL TIP: banking hours normally Mon–Fri 8:30–1:00 & 2:30–4:00 with late hours Thursdays and sometimes Fridays closing 5:30; bank holidays see* **public**

bar die Bar
barber der (Herren)friseur [(. . .)free-z*ur*]
bargain: it's a real bargain das ist wirklich
  günstig [dass isst virk-lish g*oo*n-sti*k*]
bartender der Barkeeper
basket der Korb [korp]
bassinet die Baby-Tragetasche
  [baby-trah-gheh-tash-uh]
bath das Bad [baht]
  can I have a bath? kann ich ein Bad
  nehmen? [kan ish ine baht n*ay*-men]
  could you give me a bath towel? könnten
  Sie mir ein Badetuch geben? [k*ur*rnten zee
  meer ine b*a*h-duh-too*k* g*ay*-ben]
bathing suit der Badeanzug [b*a*h-duh-an-ts*oo*g]
bathrobe der Bademantel [bah-duh–]
bathroom das Badezimmer [b*a*h-duh-tsimmer]
  we want a room with a private bathroom
  wir hätten gerne ein Zimmer mit Bad [veer
  hetten g*ai*rn-uh ine tsimmer mit baht]
  can I use your bathroom? darf ich bitte mal
  Ihre Toilette benutzen? [darf ish bittuh mal
  ee-ruh twa-lettuh buh-n*oo*tsen]
» *TRAVEL TIP: see* **toilet**
battery die Batterie
be: to be sein [zine]
  don't be angry seien Sie nicht böse [zy-en zee
  nisht burr-zuh]
  be reasonable seien Sie vernünftig! [zy-en zee
  fair-n*oo*nfti*k*]
beach der Strand [shtrannt]
beans die Bohnen [b*o*h-nen]
beautiful schön [shurrn]
  that was a beautiful meal das Essen war
  ausgezeichnet [. . . var *o*wss-gheh-tsy*k*net]
because weil [vile]
  because of the delay wegen der Verspätung
  [vayghen dair fair-sp*a*yt-*oo*ng]
bed ein Bett; **single bed/double bed** ein
  Einzelbett/Doppelbett [. . . ine-tsel-bett . . .]
  I'm off to bed ich geh'ins Bett [ish gay inz]

bed and breakfast Zimmer mit Frühstück
[tsimmer mit frōō-shtōck]
bedroom das Schlafzimmer [shlahf-tsimmer]
bee eine Biene [bee-nuh]
beef das Rindfleisch [rinnt-flysh]
beer ein Bier [beer]
  two beers, please zwei Bier, bitte [tsvy beer
  bittuh]
  YOU MAY THEN HEAR...
  Pils oder Export *Pils or Export (Pils is
  stronger)*
  große oder kleine *large or small (large = 0.5
  liter, small = 0.2)*
  eine Halbe *=½ liter = 0.9 pint*
  eine Maß *typical in Bavaria = 1 liter; if you
  like a darker beer try "ein Alt," though this is
  not available in all parts of Germany*
before: before breakfast vor dem Frühstück
[for daym frōō-shtōck]
  before we leave bevor wir gehen [buh-for veer
  gay-en]
  I haven't been here before ich bin hier noch
  nie gewesen [ish bin heer no*k* nee
  gheh-vay-zen]
begin: when does it begin? wann fängt es an?
[van fengt...]
beginner der Anfänger [*a*n-fenger]
beginner's slope *(skiing)* der Idiotenhügel
[id-ee-oh-ten-hōō-ghel]
behind hinter
Belgian belgisch [bel-ghish] *(person)* Belgier
[bel-gheer] *(woman)* Belgierin
Belgium Belgien [bel-ghee-un]
believe: I don't believe you das glaub' ich
Ihnen nicht [dass glōwp ish ee-nen nisht]
  I believe you ich glaub' Ihnen [ish glōwp
  ee-nen]
bell *(in hotel, etc.)* die Klingel
belong: that belongs to me das gehört mir
[dass gheh-h*u*rrt meer]

whom does this belong to? wem gehört das?
[vaym gheh-h*u*rrt dass]
below unter [*oo*nter]
belt der Gürtel [g*ōō*rtel]
bend *(in road)* die Kurve [koor-vuh]
berries die Beeren [bay-ren]
berth *(on ship)* das Bett
***besetzt** (toilet) occupied (bus) full*
beside neben [nay-ben]
best beste [best-uh]
   it's the best vacation I've ever had das ist
   der schönste Urlaub meines Lebens
   [. . . shurrn-stuh *oo*r-l*ōw*p mine-es l*a*y-benz]
***Betreten des Rasens verboten** keep off the grass*
***Betreten verboten** no trespassing*
better besser
   haven't you got anything better? haben Sie
   nichts Besseres? [h*a*h-ben zee nix . . .]
   are you feeling better? geht es Ihnen besser?
   [gayt ess ee-nen besser]
   I'm feeling a lot better es geht mir viel
   besser [ess gayt meer feel besser]
between zwischen [tsvishen]
***bewachter Parkplatz** supervised parking lot*
beyond über [*ōō*ber]
bicycle ein Fahrrad [fahr-raht]
big groß [grohss]
   a big one ein großer [ine grohss-er]
   that's too big das ist zu groß [. . . isst tsoo . . .]
   it's not big enough das ist nicht groß genug
   [dass isst nicht grohss gheh-n*oo*g]
   have you got a bigger one? haben Sie nichts
   Größeres? [h*a*h-ben zee nix grurrss-er-es]
bikini ein Bikini
bill die Rechnung [resh-n*oo*ng]
   could I have the bill, please? zahlen, bitte!
   [ts*a*h-len bittuh]
binding *(ski)* die Bindung [–*oo*ng]
bird der Vogel [f*oh*-ghel]
birthday der Geburtstag [gheh-b*oo*rts-tahg]

it's my birthday ich habe Geburtstag
happy birthday Herzlichen Glückwunsch
(zum Geburtstag)! [hairts-lishen glöck-voonsh
tsoom gheh-boorts-tahg]
bit: just a bit nur ein bißchen [noor ine
bis-shen]
that's a bit too expensive das ist ein bißchen
zu teuer [. . . bis-shen tsoo toy-er]
just a little bit for me nur ganz wenig für
mich [noor gants vay-nik för mish]
a bit of that cake ein Stückchen von dem
Kuchen da [ine shtöök-shen fon daim
kooken . . .]
bite ein Biß [biss]; *(mosquito)* ein Stich [stik]
bitte eintreten please enter
bitte klingeln please ring
bitte klopfen please knock
bitte nicht stören please do not disturb
bitter bitter; *(apple, etc.)* sauer
[zōw-er]
black schwarz [shvarts]
he's had a blackout er ist ohnmächtig
geworden [air isst ohn-mek-tik gheh-vorden]
blanket die Decke [deck-uh]
I'd like another blanket könnte ich noch
eine Decke haben? [kurrntuh ish nok ine-uh
deck-uh hah-ben]
bleach das Bleichmittel [blysh–]
bleed bluten [blooten]
bless you *(after sneeze)* Gesundheit!
[gheh-zoont-hyte]
blind blind [blinnt]; **blind spot** der tote Winkel
[dair toh-tuh vinkel]
his lights were blinding me seine
Scheinwerfer haben mich geblendet [zine-uh
shine-vairfer hah-ben mish gheh– . . .]
blister eine Blase [blah-zuh]
blocked *(pipe)* verstopft [fair-shtopft] *(road)*
blockiert [block-eert]
blond eine Blondine [blond-ee-nuh]
blood das Blut [bloot]

his blood type is... er hat Blutgruppe...
[air hat bloot-grœp-uh...]
I've got high blood pressure ich habe hohen
Blutdruck [ish hah-buh hoh-en bloot-drœck]
he needs a blood transfusion er braucht
eine Bluttransfusion [air brœwkt ine-uh
bloot-tranz-fooz-ee-ohn]
Bloody Mary eine Bloody Mary
blouse die Bluse [bloo-zuh]
blue blau [blōw]
board: full board Vollpension [foll penz-ee-ohn];
half board Halbpension [halp—]
boarding pass die Bordkarte [bort-kartuh]
boat das Boot [boht] *(bigger)* das Schiff [shiff]
boat train die Zugfähre [tsōog-fair-uh]
body der Körper [kurrper]
(dead body) eine Leiche [lysh-uh]
boil *(verb)* kochen [kok-en]; *(on skin)* ein
Furunkel [fœr-œnkel]
boiled egg gekochtes Ei [gheh-koktes eye]
bone der Knochen [kuh-noken]
(fish) die Gräte [grayt-uh]
book das Buch [book]
bookstore eine Buchhandlung [book-hant-lœng]
boot der Stiefel [shteefel]
border die Grenze [grents-uh]
bored: I'm bored mir ist langweilig [meer isst
lang-vile-ik]
boring langweilig [lang-vile-ik]
born: I was born in... ich bin in...geboren
[ish bin in...gheh-bor-ren] *see* **date**
boss der Chef
both beide [by-duh]
I'll take both of them ich nehme beide [ish
nay-muh by-duh]
bottle die Flasche [flash-uh]
bottle opener der Flaschenöffner
[flash-en-urrfner]
bottom: at the bottom of the hill unten am
Berg [œnten...]
bouncer der Rausschmeißer [rōwss-shmysser]

bowl die Schale
box die Schachtel [shah*k*tel] *(wood)* die Kiste
   [kistuh]
boy ein Junge [yŏonguh]
boyfriend der Freund [froynt]
bra der BH [b*a*y-h*a*h]
bracelet das Armband [−bannt]
brake die Bremse [brem-zuh]
   could you check the brakes? könnten Sie
   die Bremsen nachsehen? [k*u*rrnten zee dee
   brem-zen n*a*hk-zay-en]
   I had to brake suddenly ich mußte plötzlich
   bremsen [ish m*oo*stuh plurrts-lish brem-zen]
   he didn't brake er hat nicht gebremst [air
   hat nisht gheh-bremst]
brandy der Weinbrand [vine-brannt]
bread das Brot [broht]
   could we have some bread and butter?
   könnten wir etwas Brot und Butter haben?
   [k*u*rrnten veer etvass broht *oo*nt b*oo*ter
   h*a*h-ben]
   some more bread, please noch etwas Brot,
   bitte [n*o*k etvass broht bittuh]
break brechen [breshen]
   I think I've broken my arm ich glaube, ich
   habe mir den Arm gebrochen [. . . glōwbuh ish
   h*a*h-buh meer . . . gheh-bro*k*en]
breakdown die Panne [pan-uh]
   I've had a breakdown mein Wagen ist
   stehengeblieben [mine vah-ghen isst
   shtay-en-gheh-bleeben]
   nervous breakdown Nerven-zusammenbruch
   [n*a*irven-tsoo-zammen-bro*k*]
 » *TRAVEL TIP: highway patrols give free help
   (except parts); telephone for "Straßenwachthilfe"*
   [shtrahss-en-vah*k*t-hilfuh]
breakfast das Frühstück [frō-stŏock]
   English/Continental breakfast englisches/
   kleines Frühstück [. . . kline-es . . .]
breast die Brust [br*oo*st]

breath der Atem [ah-tem]
   out of breath außer Atem [ōwsser . . .]
breathe atmen [aht-men]
   I can't breathe ich bekomme keine Luft [ish
   buh-kommuh kine-uh lωft]
bridge die Brücke [brōckuh]
briefcase die (Akten)mappe [(. . .)mappuh]
brilliant *(very good)* großartig [grohss-ahrti*k*]
bring bringen
   could you bring it to my hotel? könnten Sie
   es mir ins Hotel bringen? [kurrnten zee ess
   meer ints . . .]
Britain Großbritannien [grohss-bri-t*a*hn-ee-un]
British britisch [br*ee*-tish]
   the British die Briten [br*ee*-ten]
   I'm British ich bin Brite; *(woman)* Britin
   [br*ee*-tuh; br*ee*-tin]
brochure der Prospekt
   have you got any brochures about . . . ?
   haben Sie Prospekte über . . . ?
   [h*a*h-ben zee . . . ōber]
broken kaputt
   you've broken it Sie haben es kaputt
   gemacht [zee h*a*h-ben ess . . . gheh-mah*k*t]
   my room/car has been broken into man hat
   in mein Zimmer eingebrochen/man hat meinen
   Wagen aufgebrochen [. . . mine tsimmer
   ine-gheh-bro*k*en/ . . . mine-en vah-ghen
   ōwf-gheh-bro*k*en]
brooch die Brosche [broh-shuh]
brother: my brother mein Bruder [mine
   brooder]
brown braun [br*ō*wn]
   brown paper das Packpapier [–pap*ee*r]
browse: can I just browse around? kann ich
   mich mal umsehen? [kan ish mish mal
   ωm-zay-en]
bruise ein blauer Fleck [ine bl*ō*w-er . . .]
brunette eine Brünette [ine-uh brω-nettuh]
brush die Bürste [bōrstuh] *(artist's)* der Pinsel
Brussels sprouts der Rosenkohl [roh-zen-kohl]

bucket der Eimer [eye-mer]
buffet das Büffet [bœf-ay] *(rail)* der Speisewagen
  [shpyzuh-vah-ghen]
building das Gebäude [gheh-boy-duh]
bump: he bumped his head er hat sich den
  Kopf angeschlagen [air hat zish dayn kopf
  an-gheh-shlah-ghen]
bumper die Stoßstange [shtohss-shtang-uh]
bunk das Bett; *(in ship)* die Koje [koh-yuh]
  bunk beds ein Etagenbett [ay-tahj-en−]
buoy die Boje [boh-yuh]
burglar ein Einbrecher [ine-breker]
burned: this meat is burned das Fleisch ist
  angebrannt [flysh isst an-gheh-brannt]
  my arms are burned ich habe Sonnenbrand
  an den Armen [ish hah-buh zonnen-brannt . . .]
  **can you give me something for these
  burns?** können Sie mir etwas für diese
  Brandwunden geben? [kurrnen zee meer etvass
  foor deez-uh brannt-voonden gay-ben]
bus der Bus [bœss]
  bus stop die Bushaltestelle
  [bœss-haltuh-shtelluh]
  could you tell me when we get there?
  können Sie mir sagen, wo ich aussteigen muß?
  [kurrnen zee meer zah-ghen voh ish
  öwss-shty-ghen mœss]
  » *TRAVEL TIP: on town bus routes you may have to
  buy your ticket from a machine near the bus
  stop before you get on the bus*
business das Geschäft [gheh-sheft]
  I'm here on business ich bin geschäftlich
  hier [ish bin gheh-sheft-lish heer]
  business trip eine Geschäftsreise [ine-uh
  gheh-shefts-ry-zuh]
  that's none of your business das geht Sie
  nichts an [dass gayt zee nix an]
bust die Büste [bœstuh] *(measurement)* die
  Oberweite [ohber-vy-tuh]
  (bankrupt) pleite [ply-tuh]

channel: the Channel der Ärmelkanal
[airmel-kanal]

charge: what do you charge? was verlangen
Sie? [vass fair-langen zee]
  who's in charge? wer hat hier die
Verant-wortung? [vair hat heer dee
fair-ant-vort-oong]

chart *(flowchart, etc.)* das Diagramm
[dee-ah-grahm]

cheap billig [billik]; **something cheaper** etwas
Billegeres [etvass billig-er-es]

cheat: I've been cheated ich bin betrogen
worden [ish bin buh-troh-ghen vorden]

check *(noun)* der Scheck [sheck]
  may I have the check, please? zahlen, bitte!
[tsahlen bittuh]
  will you take a check? nehmen Sie Schecks?
[nay-men zee shecks]
  checkbook das Scheckbuch [sheck-book]

check *(verb)*: **will you check?** sehen Sie bitte
nach [zay-en zee bittuh nahk]
  I've checked ich habe nachgeprüft [ish
hah-buh nahk-gheh-prööft]
  will you check the total? könnten Sie das
nachrechen? [kurrnten zee das nahk-resh-nen]
  we checked in/we checked out wir haben
uns angemeldet/abgemeldet [veer hah-ben
oonts angheh-meldet/app-gheh-meldet]

cheek die Backe [back-uh]

cheers Prost! [prohst]
  (thank you) vielen Dank [feelen . . .]

cheese der Käse [kay-zuh]
  cheesecake der Käsekuchen [–kooken]
  say cheese bitte recht freundlich [bittuh rekt
froynt-lish]

chef der Koch [kok]

chest die Brust [broost]

» *TRAVEL TIP: chest measurements*

US	34	36	38	40	42	44	46
Germany	*87*	*91*	*97*	*102*	*107*	*112*	*117*

....

chicken ein Hähnchen [hayn-shen]
chicken pox die Windpocken [vintpocken]
child ein Kind [kint]
   children die Kinder [kinder]
   children's portion ein Kinderteller
chin das Kinn
china das Porzellan [ports-ell*a*n]
chips *(in casino)* die Chips
chocolate die Schokolade [shok-oh-l*a*hduh]
   hot chocolate (heiße) Schokolade [hyssuh]
   a box of chocolates Pralinen [prah-l*ee*nen]
choke *(car)* der Choke
chop ein Kotelett [kot-lett]
   pork/lamb chop Schweine-/Lammkotelett
Christmas Weihnachten [vy-nah*k*-ten]
   Merry Christmas fröhliche Weihnachten
   [frurrlish-uh . . .]
   Christmas Eve Heiligabend [hile-i*k*-*a*hbent]
» *TRAVEL TIP: Christmas in Germany starts on the*
   24th (Heiligabend) when work normally stops
   at midday; presents are given on the evening of
   the 24th; holidays on Christmas Day (der erste
   Weihnachtstag) and Boxing Day (der zweite
   Weihnachtstag); on December 6th children find
   candy and nuts put in their shoes during the
   night by St. Nikolaus
church die Kirche [k*ee*r-shuh]
   where is the Protestant/Catholic church?
   wo ist die evangelische/katholische Kirche?
   [voh ist dee . . .]
cider der Apfelmost
cigar die Zigarre [tsig*a*rruh]
cigarette die Zigarette [tsigarr-ettuh]
   would you like a cigarette? darf ich Ihnen
   eine Zigarette anbieten? [. . . ish een-en ine-uh
   tsigarr-*e*ttuh an-bee-ten]
» *TRAVEL TIP: don't be offended if you're not*
   offered a cigarette; normally people smoke their
   own
circle der Kreis [krice]
city die Stadt [shtatt]

claim *(insurance)* der Anspruch [*a*n-shpr∞k]
clarify klären [klairen]
clean *(adjective)* sauber [zōwber]
    can I have some clean sheets? kann ich
    frische Bettwäsche haben? [kann ish frish-uh
    bett-vesh-uh h*a*h-ben]
    my room hasn't been cleaned today in
    meinem Zimmer ist heute nicht
    saubergemacht worden [in mine-em tsimmer
    isst hoy-tuh nisht zōwber-gheh-mah*k*t vorden]
it's not clean das ist nicht sauber
clear klar
    I'm not clear about it ich bin mir darüber
    nicht im klaren [ish bin meer dar∞ber
    nisht . . .]
clear up: do you think it'll clear up later?
    glauben Sie, es klärt sich später auf?
    [glōwben zee es klairt zish spayter ōwf]
clever klug [kloog] *(skillful)* geschickt
    [gheh-shickt]
climate das Klima [kl*ee*-mah]
climb: we're going to climb . . . wir
    besteigen . . . [veer buh-shty-ghen]
    climber ein Bergsteiger [bairk-shty-gher]
    climbing boots die Bergstiefel [– shteefel]
clip *(ski: on boot)* die Schnalle [shnall-uh]
clock die Uhr [oor]
close¹: nahe [nah-uh]
close²: when do you close? wann machen Sie
    zu? [van mah*k*en zee tsoo]
closed geschlossen [gheh-shlossen]
cloth das Tuch [too*k*]
clothes die Kleider [kly-der]
    clothespin die Wäscheklammer [vesh-uh –]
cloud die Wolke [vol-kuh]
clutch die Kupplung [k∞p-l∞ng]
    the clutch is slipping die Kupplung schleift
    [. . . shlyft]
coast die Küste [k∞stuh]
    coastguard die Küstenwache
    [k∞sten-vah*k*-uh]

coat der Mantel
coatroom die Garderobe [garduh-robe-uh]
cockroach eine Küchenschabe [kōken-shah-buh]
coffee ein Kaffee [kaffay]
 white coffee/black coffee Kaffee mit Milch/
 Kaffee schwarz [. . . mit milsh/ . . . shvarts]
 two coffees, please zwei Kaffee, bitte [tsvy
 kaffay bittuh]
 YOU MAY THEN HEAR . . .
 Kännchen oder Tassen? *pots or cups?* [ken-shen
 oh-der . . .] *a pot is usually 2 cups; coffee and
 cream are always served separately*
coin die Münze [mōon-tsuh]
cold kalt
 I'm cold ich friere [ish free-ruh]
 I've got a cold ich bin erkältet [ish bin
 air-keltet]
collapse: he's collapsed er ist
 zusammen-gebrochen [air isst
 tsoo-zammen-gheh-broken]
collar der Kragen [krah-ghen]
 collarbone das Schlüsselbein [shlōossel-bine]
» *TRAVEL TIP: sizes*
  US: 14 14½ 15 15½ 16 16½ 17
  continental: 36 37   38 39   41 42   43
collect abholen [app-hoh-len]
 can I collect my shirts? ich möchte meine
 Hemden abholen [ish murrshtuh mine-uh . . .]
collision der Zusammenstoß
 [tsoo-zammen-shtohss]
color die Farbe [far-buh]
 have you any other colors? haben Sie noch
 andere Farben? [hah-ben zee nok ander-uh
 far-ben]
comb ein Kamm
come kommen
 I come from London ich komme aus London
 [ish kommuh ōwss . . .]
 we came here yesterday wir sind gestern
 hier angekommen [veer zint ghestern heer
 an-gheh-kommen]

when is he coming? wann kommt er? [van kommt air]
come on! komm!
come with me kommen Sie mit! [... zee ...]
comfortable bequem [buh-kvaym]
it's not very comfortable es ist nicht sehr bequem [... nisht zayr buh-kvaym]
Common Market die EWG [ay-vay-gay]
company die Gesellschaft [gheh-zell-shafft]
you're good company ich bin gern mit Ihnen zusammen [ish bin gairn mit ee-nen tsoo-zammen]
compartment *(train)* das Abteil [app-tile]
compass der Kompaß [kom-pas]
compensation die Entschädigung [ent-shayd-ee-gœng]
I demand compensation ich verlange Schadenersatz [ish fair-lang-uh shaden-airsats]
complain sich beschweren [zish buh-shvairen]
I want to complain about the waiter ich möchte mich über den Kellner beschweren [ish murrshtuh mish ōber dayn kellner ...]
have you got a complaints book? das Beschwerdebuch, bitte! [dass buh-shvair-duh-book bittuh]
completely völlig [furrlik]
complicated: it's very complicated es ist sehr kompliziert [... zair komplits-eert]
compliment das Kompliment [−ment]
my compliments to the chef mien Lob der Küche [mine lohp dair kōōk-uh]
concert das Konzert [kontsairt]
concussion eine Gehirnerschütterung [gheh-hirn-air-shōōt-erœng]
condition die Bedingung [buh-ding-œng]
it's not in very good condition es ist nicht in besonders gutem Zustand [... nisht in buh-zonders gootem tsoo-shtant]
condom ein Kondom [kon-dōhm]
conference die Konferenz [kon-fer-ents]
confession das Geständnis [gheh-shtent-nis]

confirm bestätigen [buh-st*ay*t-ee-g*oo*ng]
confuse: you're confusing me Sie bringen
  mich durcheinander [zee bringen mish
  d*oo*rsh-ine-ander]
congratulations! herzlichen Glückwunsch!
  [hairts-lishen gl*oo*ck-v*oo*nsh]
conjunctivitis die Bindehautentzündung
  [binduh-h*oo*wt-ent-ts*oo*n-d*oo*ng]
con man der Schwindler [shvintler]
connection die Verbindung [fair-b*i*n-d*oo*ng]
connoisseur der Kenner
conscious bewußt [buh-v*oo*st]
consciousness: he's lost consciousness er ist
  bewußtlos [air ist buh-v*oo*sst-lohs]
constipation die Verstopfung [fair-sht*o*p-*oo*ng]
consul der Konsul [kon-z*oo*l]
consulate das Konsulat [kon-z*oo*l-*ah*t]
contact: how can I contact . . . ? wie kann
  ich . . . erreichen? [vee kann ish . . . air-ryshen]
  I'll get in contact soon ich werde mich
  melden [ish vairduh mish . . .]
  contact lens die Kontaktlinsen [−zen]
contraceptive ein empfängnisverhütendes
  Mittel [emp-feng-nis-fair-h*oo*t-end-ess . . .]
convenient günstig [g*oo*nstik]
cook: it's not cooked es ist nicht gar
  it was beautifully cooked das war
  vorzüglich [dass var for-ts*oo*g-lish]
  you're a good cook Sie kochen ausgezeichnet
  [zee ko*k*en *oo*wss-gheh-tsy*k*-net]
cookie ein keks
cool kühl [k*oo*l]
corkscrew der Korkenzieher [−tsee-er]
corn *(foot)* ein Hühnerauge [h*oo*ner-*oo*wg-uh]
corner die Ecke [eck-uh]
  can we have a corner table? können wir
  einen Ecktisch haben? [k*u*rrnen veer ine-en
  eck-tish h*ah*-ben]
cornflakes die Cornflakes
correct richtig [r*i*k-ti*k*]
cosmetics die Kosmetika [kosm*ay*tikah]

cost: what does it cost? was kostet das? [vass kostet dass]
  that's too much das ist zu viel [dass isst tsoo feel]
  I'll take it ich nehme es [ish nay-muh ess]
cotton die Baumwolle [bówm-volluh]
couchette der Liegesitz [leeg-uh-zits]
cough der Husten [hoosten]
  cough drops die Hustentropfen
  cough mixture der Hustensaft [−zaft]
could: could you please... könnten Sie, bitte,...? [kurrnten zee bittuh...]
  could I have...? dürfte ich...haben? [dōōrf-tuh ish...hah-ben]
  we couldn't... wir konnten nicht... [veer]
country das Land [lannt]
  in the country auf dem Land [ōwf daym lannt]
couple: a couple of... ein paar... [ine pahr]
courier der Reiseleiter [ry-zuh-ly-ter]
course *(of meal)* der Gang
  of course natürlich [natōōr-lish]
court: I'll take you to court ich werde Sie vor Gericht bringen [ish vair-duh zee for gheh-rikt...]
cousin der Cousin; die Cousine [koo-zan koo-zeen-uh]
cover: keep him covered decken Sie ihn zu [...zee een tsoo]
  cover charge ein Gedeck [gheh-deck]
cow die Kuh [koo]
crab die Krabbe [krabbuh]
crash: there's been a crash da ist ein Unfall passiert [da isst ine ōōn-fal pas-eert]
crazy verrückt [fair-rōōckt]
  you're crazy du spinnst [doo shpinnst]
cream die Sahne [zah-nuh] *(with butter)* die Creme [kray-muh]
  (for skin) die Creme
  (color) cremefarben [−far-ben]
credit card die Kreditkarte [kredeet-kartuh]

crib die Kinderkrippe [kinder-krippuh]
crisis die Krise [kree-zuh]
crossroads die Kreuzung [kroytsoong]
crowded überfüllt [ober-foolt]
cruise die Bootsfahrt [bohts-fahrt]
crutch die Krücke [krook-uh]
cry: don't cry weinen Sie nicht [vine-en zee nisht]
cup die Tasse [tass-uh]; **a cup of coffee** eine Tasse Kaffee [ine-uh tass-uh kaffay]
cupboard der Schrank [shrank]
curry der Curry
curtains der Vorhang [for-hang]
cushion das Kissen
Customs der Zoll [tsoll]
cut: I've cut myself ich habe mich geschnitten [ish hah-buh mish gheh-schnitten]
cycle: can we cycle there? können wir mit dem Rad dorthin fahren? [kurrnen veer mit daym raht dort-hin far-ren]
　　cyclist der Radfahrer [raht-far-rer]
cylinder der Zylinder [tsoolinder]
　　cylinder head gasket die Zylinderkopf-dichtung [tsoolinder-kopf-dik-toong]
dad(dy) der Papa
damage: I'll pay for the damage ich werde für den Schaden aufkommen [ish vair-duh foor dayn shahden owf-kommen]
　　it's damaged es ist beschädigt [es isst buh-shayd-ikt]
Damen Ladies' room
damn! verdammt! [fair-dammt]
damp feucht [foysht]
dance: is there a dance on? ist da Tanz?
　　would you like to dance? möchten Sie tanzen? [murrshten zee tantsen]
dangerous gefährlich [gheh-fair-lish]
dark dunkel [doonkel]
　　when does it get dark? wann wird es dunkel? [van virt ess doonkel]
　　dark blue dunkelblau [doonkel-blow]

darling Liebling [leep-ling]
dashboard das Armaturenbrett [−tooren−]
date: what's the date? der wievielte ist heute?
[dair vee-*feel*-tuh isst h*oy*-tuh]
   can we fix a date? können wir einen Termin
   abmachen? [k*u*rrnen veer ine-en tair-m*ee*n
   app-mah*k*en]
   on the fifth of May am fünften Mai [am
   f*oo*nften my]
   in 1951 neunzehnhunderteinundfünfzig
   [noyn-tsayn-h*oo*ndert-ine-*oo*nt-f*oo*nf-tsi*k*]
» *TRAVEL TIP: to say the date in German add
   letters "ten" to the number if 1–19, and "sten" if
   20–31; see numbers on p. 127; exceptions:*
   first ersten; **third** dritten; **seventh** siebten
daughter: my daughter meine Tochter
   [mine-uh to*k*ter]
day der Tag [tahg]
dead tot [toht]
deaf taub [t*ō*wp]
deal *(business)* das Geschäft [gheh-sh*e*ft]
   it's a deal abgemacht [app-gheh-mah*k*t]
   will you deal with it? kümmern Sie sich,
   bitte, darum? [k*ō*m-ern zee zish bittuh
   da-r*oo*m]
Dear Mr. Kunz Sehr geehrter Herr Kunz
Dear Franz Lieber Franz
Dear Sir *if no name known, write:* Sehr geehrte
   Damen und Herren
December Dezember [dayts−]
deck das Deck
   deckchair der Liegestuhl [leeguh-shtool]
declare: nothing to declare nichts zu verzollen
   [nix tsoo fair-tsollen]
deep tief [teef]
defendant der Angeklagte [*a*n-gheh-klahg-tuh]
   (in civil cases) der Beklagte [buh−]
delay: the flight was delayed der Flug hatte
   Verspätung [dair floog hat-uh fair-shp*ay*t-*oo*ng]
deliberately absichtlich [*a*pp-zisht-lish]
delicate *(person)* zart [tsart]

delicatessen ein Delikatessengeschäft
[−gheh-sheft]
delicious köstlich [kurrst-lish]
delivery der Lieferung [leeferoong]
  is there another mail delivery? gibt es noch
  eine Zustellung? [gheept ess nok ine-uh
  tsoo-shtel-oong]
deluxe Luxus− [looxooss]
democratic demokratisch [−krah-tish]
demonstration *(of gadget)* eine Vorführung
[for-fōōr-roong]
dent die Delle [delluh]
  you've dented my car Sie haben mir mein
  Auto eingedellt [zee hah-ben meer
  mine ōw-toh ine-gheh-dellt]
dentist der Zahnarzt [tsahn-arst]
  YOU MAY HEAR...
  bitte weit öffnen *open wide*
  bitte ausspülen *rinse out*
dentures das Gebiß [gheh-biss] *(partial)* die
Zahnprothese [tsahn-proh-tay-zuh]
deny: I deny it das bestreite ich [dass
buh-shtry-tuh ish]
deodorant das Deodorant [day−]
departure die Abreise [app-ry-zuh]
  (bus, train) die Abfahrt
  (plane) der Abflug [app-floog]
depend: it depends das kommt darauf an
[...da-rōwf...]
  it depends on him das kommt auf ihn an
deport deportieren [−ee-ren]
deposit die Anzahlung [antsah-loong]
  do I have to leave a deposit? muß ich eine
  Kaution hinterlegen? [mooss ish ine-uh
  kōw-tsee-ohn hinterlay-ghen]
depressed deprimiert [day-prim-eert]
depth die Tiefe [teefuh]
desperate: I'm desperate for a drink ich
brauche dringend was zu trinken [ish brōwkuh
dringent...tsoo...]
dessert der Nachtisch [nahk−]

destination das Reiseziel [ry-zuh-tseel]
  (of goods) der Bestimmungsort
  [buh-shtim-oongs-ort]
detergent das Waschmittel
detour der Umweg [oom-vegg]
devalued abgewertet [app-gheh-vairtet]
develop: could you develop these? könnten
  Sie diese entwickeln? [kurrnten zee dee-zuh
  ent-v–]
diabetic ein Diabetiker [dee–] *(woman)* eine
  Diabetikerin
  (adjective) diabetisch [dee-ah-bay-tish]
dialing code die Vorwahl [for-vahl]
diamond der Diamant [dee–]
diaper der Windel [vindel]
diarrhea der Durchfall [doorsh-fal]
  have you got something for diarrhea?
  haben Sie ein Mittel gegen Durchfall?
  [hah-ben zee . . .]
diary das Tagebuch [tah-ghen-book]
dictionary ein Wörterbuch [vurr-ter-book]
die sterben [shtairben]
  he's dying er stirbt [air shteerbt]
diesel *(fuel)* Diesel
diet die Diät [dee-ayt]
  I'm on a diet ich mache eine Schlankheitskur
  [ish mahk-uh ine-uh shlank-hites-koor]
different: they are different sie sind
  verschieden [zee zint fair-shee-den]
  can I have a different room? kann ich ein
  anderes Zimmer haben? [ine an-der-es . . .]
  is there a different route? gibt es eine
  andere Strecke?
difficult schwierig [shveerik]
digestion die Verdauung [fair-dow-oong]
dinghy das Ding(h)i; *(collapsible)* das
  Schlauchboot [shlowk-boht]
dining room das Eßzimmer [ess-tsimmer]
  (in hotel) der Speiseraum [shpy-zuh-rowm]
dining car *(train)* der Speisewagen
  [shpyzuh-vah-ghen]

dinner *(evening)* das (Abend)essen [ah-bent−]
  (lunch) das (Mittag)essen [mittahg]
  dinner jacket die Smokingjacke [−yackuh]
direct *(adjective)* direkt [dee−]
  does it go direct? ist es eine
  Direkt-verbindung? [ine-uh
  deerekt-fairbindoong]
dirty schmutzig [shmootsik]
disabled behindert [buh-hinndert]
disappear verschwinden [fair-schvinnden]
  it's just disappeared es ist einfach
  verschwunden [ess isst ine-fahk fair-shvoonden]
disappointing enttäuschend [ent-toyshent]
disco die Disko
discount der Rabatt
  cash discount Skonto
disgusting widerlich [veeder-lish]
dish *(food)* das Gericht [geh-risht]
  (plate) die Schüssel [shoossel]
dishonest unehrlich [oon-airlish]
disinfectant das Desinfektionsmittel
  [days-infek-tsee-ohns−]
distance die Entfernung [ent-fair-noong]
  in the distance in der Ferne [in dair fairnuh]
distress signal ein Notsignal [noht-zignahl]
distributor *(car)* der Verteiler [fair-tyler]
disturb: the noise is disturbing us der Lärm
  stört uns [dair lairm shturrt oonz]
divorced geschieden [geh-sheeden]
do machen [mahken]
  how do you do? guten Tag [gooten tahg]
  what are you doing tonight? was machen
  Sie heute abend? [vass . . . zee hoytuh ah-bent]
  how do you do it? wie machen Sie das?
  [vee . . . zee . . .]
  will you do it for me? machen Sie das für
  mich? [. . . foor mish]
  I've never done it before ich habe das noch
  nie gemacht [ish hah-buh dass nok nee
  geh-mahkt]

I was doing 60 kph ich fuhr mit 60 km/h
[ish foor mit zek-tsik]
doctor der Arzt
  I need a doctor ich brauche einen Arzt [ish
  brōwkuh ine-en . . .]
  YOU MAY HEAR . . .
  haben Sie das schon einmal gehabt? *have you
  had this before?*
  wo tut es weh? *where does it hurt?*
  nehmen Sie zur Zeit Medikamente? *are you
  taking any medication at the moment?*
  nehmen Sie eine davon dreimal/viermal
  täglich *take one of these three/four times a day*
document das Dokument [−ooment]
dog ein Hund [hoont]
don't! nicht! [nisht] *see* **not**
door die Tür [tōor]
dosage die Dosis [doh-ziss]
double: double room Doppelzimmer [−tsimmer]
  double whisky ein doppelter Whisky
down: get down! runter! [roonter]
  it's down the road es ist nur ein Stückchen
  weiter [. . . noor ine shtōōk-shen vy-ter]
  he's downstairs er ist unten [. . . oonten]
drain das (Abfluß) rohr [app-flōoss-ror]
dress das Kleid [klite]
» *TRAVEL TIP: dress sizes*
  US   6 10 12 14 16 18
  Germany 36 38 40 42 44 46
dressing *(for wound)* der Verband [fair-bannt]
  (for salad) die Sauce [zohsuh]
drink: would you like a drink? möchten Sie
  etwas trinken? [murrshten zee etvass . . .]
  I don't drink ich trinke keinen Alkohol [ish
  trinkuh kine-en al-koh-hohl]
  I had too much to drink last night ich habe
  gestern abend zu viel getrunken [ish hah-buh
  ghestern ah-bent tsoo feel gheh-troonken]
  is the water drinkable? kann man das
  Wasser trinken?

» *TRAVEL TIP: licensing hours are far less strict in Germany; drinks can be served at all hours*
drive fahren
I've been driving all day ich bin den ganzen Tag gefahren [ish ... gantsen tahg gheh−]
driver der Fahrer
driving license der Führerschein [fōrer-shine]
» *TRAVEL TIP: driving in Germany−speed limits: 50 kph (31 mph) in town; 100 (62) outside; freeways 130 (81) recommended with 60 (37) minimum; trucks and motorhomes max. 80 (49); seat belt, red triangle, and first aid kit compulsory*
drown: he's drowing er ertrinkt [air airtrinkt]
drücken *push*
drug das Medikament; *(illegal, etc.)* die Droge [droh-ghuh]
drugstore die Drogerie [drohgher-ee]
drunk *(adjective)* betrunken [buh-trœnken]
dry trocken
   dry-clean chemisch reinigen [shaymish ry-niggen]
due: when is the bus due? wann soll der Bus ankommen? [van zoll dair bœss ...]
Durchfahrt verboten *no through road*
Durchgangsverkehr *through traffic*
during während [vair-rent]
Duschen *showers*
dust der Staub [shtowp]
Dutch holländisch [hol-end-ish]
   Dutchman Holländer
   Dutchwoman Holländerin
duty-free *(noun)* das Duty-free
dynamo der Dynamo [dōn-ahmoh]
each: can we have one each? können wir jeder eins haben? [kurrnen veer yay-der ine-ts hah-ben]
   how much are they each? was kosten sie pro Stück? [vass kosten zee proh shtōk]
ear das Ohr [or]

I have an earache ich habe Ohrenschmerzen
[ish hah-buh or-ren-shmairtsen]
early früh [frōō]
   we want to leave a day earlier wir möchten
   einen Tag früher abreisen [veer murrshten
   ine-en tahg frōō-uh app-ry-zen]
earring der Ohrring [or-ring]
east der Osten
Easter Ostern [oh-stern]
easy leicht [lysht]
eat essen; **something to eat** etwas zu essen
[ett-vass tsoo . . .]
egg ein Ei [eye]
eggplant die Aubergine [−eenuh]
Einbahnstraße one-way street
Einfahrt (to) freeway
Eingang entrance
einordnen merge lane
Einstieg vorn/hinten enter at the front/rear
Eintritt frei admission free
Eire Irland [eer-lannt]
either: either . . . or . . . entweder . . . oder
[ent-vay-der oh-der]
   I don't like either mir gefällt beides nicht
   [meer gheh-fellt by-des nisht]
elastic elastisch
elbow der Ellbogen [el-boh-ghen]
electric elektrisch
   electric blanket eine Heizdecke
   [hites-deckuh]
   electric heater ein elektrisches Heizgerät
   [. . . hites-gheh-rayt]
electrical outlet die Steckdose [shteck-doh-zuh]
electrician der Elektriker
electricity die Elektrizität [elek-trits-i-tayt]
elegant elegant [el-ay-gannt]
elevator der Fahrstuhl
   the elevator isn't working der Fahrstuhl ist
   außer Betrieb [. . . fahr-shtool isst ōwsser
   buh-treep]
else: something else etwas anderes [ett-vass . . .]

somewhere else irgendwo anders
[eer-ghent-voh . . .]
let's go somewhere else gehen wir woanders
hin! [gay-en veer vo . . .]
who else? wer sonst? [vair . . .]
or else sonst
embarrassed verlegen [fair-*lay*-ghen]
embarrassing peinlich [pine-lish]
embassy die Botschaft [boht-shafft]
emergency der Notfall [noht-fal]
empty leer [layr]
enclose: I enclose . . . ich lege . . . bei
end das Ende; **when does it end?** bis wann
geht es? [biss van gayt ess]
engaged *(telephone, toilet)* besetzt [buh-*zetst*]
(person) verlobt [fair-*lohbt*]
engagement ring der Verlobungsring
engine die Maschine [mash-*ee*-nuh]
(of car, plane) der Motor [moh-tor]
engine trouble Schwierigkeiten mit dem
Motor [shvee-ri*k*-kite-en mit daym . . .]
England England [eng-glannt]
English englisch
the English die Engländer [eng-glender]
I'm English ich bin Engländer
(woman) ich bin Engländerin
enjoy: I enjoyed it very much ich habe es sehr
genossen [ish h*ah*-buh ess zair gheh−]
enjoy yourself viel Spaß! [feel shpass]
I enjoy riding/driving ich reite/fahre gern
[ish ry-tuh/f*ah*-ruh gairn]
enlargement *(photo)* die Vergrößerung
[fair-gr*urrs*-er*oo*ng]
enormous enorm [ay-n*o*rm]
enough genug [gheh-noog]
thank you, that's enough danke, das reicht
[dankuh dass rysht]
entertainment die Unterhaltung
[*oo*nter-h*a*lt-*oo*ng]
entrance der Eingang [ine-gang]

entry der Eintritt [ine−]
envelope ein Umschlag [oom-shlahg]
equipment die Ausrüstung [ōws-rōost-oong]
  electrical equipment Elektrogeräte
  [−gheh-r*ay*t-uh]
Erdgeschoß *ground floor*
Erfrischungen *refreshments*
error der Fehler [fayler]
erste Hilfe *first aid*
Erwachsene *adults*
escalator die Rolltreppe [−puh]
especially besonders [buh-zonnders]
essential notwendig [noht-ven-di*k*]
  it is essential that... es ist unbedingt
  erforderlich, daß... [ess isst oon-buh-dingt
  air-ford-uh-lish dass]
Europe Europa [oy-roh-pa]
evacuate evakuieren [ay-vak-oo-*ee*-ren]
even: even the British sogar die Briten [zoh-gar
  dee bree-ten]
evening der Abend [ah-bent]
  good evening guten Abend [gooten...]
  this evening heute abend [hoytuh...]
evening dress der Abendanzug [−an-tsoog]
  (woman's) das Abendkleid [−klite]
ever: have you ever been to...? sind Sie
  jemals in... gewesen? [zinnt zee yay-malz
  in... gheh-vay-zen]
every jeder [yay-duh]
  every day jeden Tag [yay-den tahg]
everyone jeder
  is everyone ready? sind alle fertig? [zinnt
  al-uh fair-ti*k*]
  everything alles [al-less]
  everywhere überall [ōober-al]
evidence der Beweis [buh-vice]
exact(ly) genau [gheh-n*ow*]
example das Beispiel [by-shpeel]
  for example zum Beispiel [tsoom...]
excellent ausgezeichnet [*ō*wss-gheh-tsysh-net]

except: except me außer mir [ṓwss-uh meer]
excess: excess baggage Übergewicht
[ōober-gheh-visht]
    excess fare die Nachlösegebühr
[nah*k*-lurr-zuh-gheh-bōor]
exchange *(money)* die Wechselstube
[vek-sel-shtoo-buh]
exciting aufregend [ṓwf-ray-ghent]
excursion der Ausflug [ṓwss-floog]
    excursion ticket verbilligte Fahrkarte
[fair-bill-i*k*tuh fahr-kartuh]
excuse: excuse me entschuldigen Sie!
[ent-shōol-dig-en zee]
exhaust *(car)* der Auspuff [ṓwss-pōof]
exhausted erschöpft [air-shupft]
exhibition die Ausstellung [ṓwss-shtel-ōong]
exhibitor der Aussteller [ṓwss-shteller]
exit der Ausgang [ṓwss-gang]
expect erwarten [air-v*a*rten]
    she's expecting sie ist in anderen Umständen
[zee isst in an-duh-ren ōom-shtenden]
expenses die Kosten
    it's on an expense account das geht auf
Spesen [dass gayt ṓwf shp*a*y-zen]
expensive teuer [toy-er]
expert der Experte [−pair-tuh]
explain erklären [air-kl*ai*ren]
    would you explain that slowly? könnten Sie
das langsam erklären? [k*u*rrnten zee dass . . .]
export *(noun)* der Export
exposure meter der Belichtungsmesser
[buh-lishtōongs−]
express *(send letter)* per Expreß [pair express]
extra zusätzlich [tsoo-zets-lish]
    an extra glass/day ein Glas/Tag extra [ine
glahss/tahg ex-trah]
    is that extra? wird das extra berechnet?
[veert dass . . . buh-r*e*sh-net]
extremely äußerst [oyss−]
eye das Auge [ṓw-guh]

eyebrow die Augenbraue [ów-ghen-brów-uh]
eyeshadow der Lidschatten [leet-shat-en]
eyewitness der Augenzeuge [−tsoy-guh]
face das Gesicht [gheh-zisht]
fact die Tatsache [taht-zahk-uh]
factory die Fabrik [fab-reek]
Fahrenheit Fahrenheit

» *TRAVEL TIP: to convert F to C:* $F - 32 \times \frac{5}{9} = C$

Fahrenheit	14	23	32	50	59	70	86	98.4
centigrade	−10	−5	0	10	15	21	30	36.9

Fahrkarten tickets
faint: she's fainted sie ist ohnmächtig geworden
[zee isst ohn-mesh-tik gheh-vorden]
fair *(fun−)* der Jahrmarkt [yah−]
   (commercial) die Messe [mess-uh]
   that's not fair das ist nicht fair
faithfully: yours faithfully hochachtungsvoll
fake *(noun)* eine Fälschung [fell-shoong]
fall fallen [fal-en]
   he's fallen er ist gefallen [air isst gheh−]
false falsch
family die Familie [fam-ee-lee-uh]
fan der Ventilator [−ah-tor]
   (football, etc.) der Fan [fen]
   fan belt der Keilriemen [kile-ree-men]
far weit [vite]
   is it far? ist es weit? [isst ess vite]
   how far is it? wie weit ist es? [vee . . .]
fare *(travel)* der Fahrpreis [fahr-price]
   (on plane) der Flugpreis [floog-price]
farm der Bauernhof [bów-ern-hohf]
farther weiter [vy−]
fashion die Mode [moh-duh]
fast schnell
   don't speak so fast sprechen Sie nicht so
   schnell! [shpreshen zee nisht zoh . . .]
fat dick *(noun)* das Fett
fatally tödlich [turrt-lish]
father: my father mein Vater [mine fah−]

faucet der Hahn
fault der Fehler [fayler]
  it's not my fault das ist nicht meine Schuld
  [dass isst nisht mine-uh-shoolt]
faulty defekt [dayfekt]
favorite *(adjective)* Lieblings– [leep-lings]
  my favorite city meine Lieblingsstadt
  [mine-uh leep-lings-shtatt]
February Februar [fay-broo-ar]
fed up: I'm fed up ich habe die Nase voll [ish
  hah-buh dee nah-zuh foll]
feel: I feel cold/hot/sad mir ist kalt/heiß/ich bin
  irgendwie traurig [meer isst kalt/hice/ish bin
  eer-ghent-vee trōw-rik]
  I feel like . . . ich habe Lust auf . . . [ish
  hah-buh loost ōwf]
Feierabend! we're closing
Fernsprecher telephone
ferry die Fähre [fay-ruh]
Feuermelder fire alarm
fever das Fieber [feeber]
  he's got a fever er hat Fieber [air hat feeber]
few wenige [vay-nig-uh]
  only a few nur ein paar [noor ine pahr]
  a few days ein paar Tage [ine pahr tah-guh]
fiancé: my fiancé mein Verlobter [mine
  fair-lohb-ter]
fiancée: my fiancée meine Verlobte [mine-uh
  fair-lohb-tuh]
field das Feld [fellt] *(grass)* die Wiese [vee-zuh]
fifty-fifty fifty-fifty
figure die Zahl [tsahl]
  (of person) die Figur [fig-oor]
  I'm watching my figure ich muß auf meine
  Figur achten [ish mooss ōwf mine-uh . . .
  ahk-ten]
fill füllen [fool-en]
  fill her up volltanken, bitte [foll– bittuh]
  to fill in a form ein Formular ausfüllen
  [. . . ōws-fool-en]
fillet das Filet [feelay]

filling *(tooth)* eine Plombe [plom-buh]
film der Film
  do you have this type of film? haben Sie
  solche Filme? [hah-ben zee zolshuh ...]
filter: filter or non-filter? mit Filter oder ohne?
  [... oh-der oh-nuh]
find finden [finn-den]; **if you find it ...** wenn
  Sie es finden ... [ven zee ess ...]
  I've found a ... ich habe ein ... gefunden [ish
  hah-buh ine ... gheh-foonden]
fine: fine weather schönes Wetter
  [shurrn-ess v–]
  a 50 marks fine eine Geldbuße von fünfzig
  Mark [ine-uh ghellt-boo-zuh fon fōōnf-tsik ...]
  OK, that's fine das ist gut [dass isst goot]
finger der Finger [finng-uh]
  fingernail der Fingernagel [–nah-ghel]
finish: I haven't finished ich bin noch nicht
  fertig [ish bin nok nisht fair-tik]
fire: fire! Feuer! [foy-uh]
  can we light a fire here? können wir heir
  ein Feuer anzünden? [kurrnen veer heer ine
  ... an-tsōōnden]
  fire extinguisher der Feuerlöscher
  [–lurrscher]
  fire department die Feuerwehr [–vair]
» *TRAVEL TIP: dial 112*
firm *(noun)* die Firma [feer-mah]
first erste [air-stuh]
  I was first ich war erster [ish var ...]
  first aid Erste Hilfe [... hill-fuh]
  first aid kit der Verbandskasten
  [fair-bannts–]
  first class erste Klasse [... klass-uh]
  first name der Vorname [for-nah-muh]
fish der Fisch
fishing das Angeln [ang-eln]
  fishing rod/tackle die Angelrute/das
  Angelzeug [ang-el-rootuh/–tsoyg]
fix: can you fix it? *(arrange, repair)* können Sie
  das machen? [kurrnen zee dass mahken]

....

fizzy mit Kohlensäure [mit kohlen-zoy-ruh]
flag die Fahne [fah-nuh]; *(national, ship's)* die
  Flagge [flag-uh]
flash *(photographic)* das Blitzlicht [−li*k*t]
flashlight eine Taschenlampe [tashen-lamp-uh]
flat flach [flah*k*]
  this drink is flat das schmeckt abgestanden
  [dass . . . *a*pp-gheh-shtanden]
  I've got a flat (tire) ich habe einen Platten
  [ish h*a*h-buh ine-en . . .]
flavor der Geschmack [gheh−]
flea der Floh
flight der Flug [floog]
flirt *(verb)* flirten
float schwimmen [shvimmen]
floor der Boden [boh-den]
  on the second floor im zweiten Stock
  [. . . tsvy-ten shtock]
» *TRAVEL TIP: Europeans call the second floor the
  first floor, the third floor the second floor, etc.*
flower die Blume [bloo-muh]
  bunch of flowers ein Blumenstrauß
  [bl*oo*men-shtr*ö*wss]
flu die Grippe [gr*i*p-uh]
fly *(insect)* die Fliege [fl*ee*-guh]
  (trousers) der Reißverschluß [r*i*ce-fair-shlooss]
foggy neblig [n*a*y-bli*k*]
follow folgen [foll-ghen]
  follow me folgen Sie mir [. . . zee meer]
food das Essen; *(groceries)* die Lebensmittel
  [lay-benz−]
  food poisoning Lebensmittelvergiftung
  [−fair-gh*i*f-t*oo*ng]
  see pages 72–73
fool der Narr
foot der Fuß [fooss]
» *TRAVEL TIP: 1 foot = 30.1 cm = 0.3 meters*
football Fußball [fooss-bal]
for für [f*ö*r]
forbidden verboten [fair-b*o*h-ten]
foreign ausländisch [*ö*ws-lend-ish]

foreign exchange Devisen [day-*vee*-zen]
foreigner ein Ausländer [*őws*-lender]
forest der Wald [valt]
forget vergessen [fair-gh*essen*]
   I forget, I've forgotten ich habe es vergessen
   [ish h*ah*-buh ess . . .]
   don't forget vergessen Sie nicht [. . . zee nisht]
   I'll never forget you ich werde dich nie
   vergessen [. . . v*air*-duh dish nee . . .]
fork die Gabel [g*ah*-bel]
form *(document)* das Formular [form-oo-l*a*r]
formal formell; *(person, manner)* förmlich
   [furrm-lish]
fortnight vierzehn Tage [feer-tsayn t*ah*-guh]
forward *(adverb)* vorwärts [for-vairtz]
   forwarding address die Nachsendeadresse
   [n*ah*k-zenduh-ad-ressuh]
   could you forward my mail? könnten Sie
   mir die Post nachsenden? [k*u*rrnten zee meer
   dee posst nah*k*-zenden]
foundation *(makeup)* die Grundierungscreme
   [gr*oo*n-d*ee*r-r*oo*ngs-kray-muh]
fracture der Bruch [br*oo*k]
fragile zerbrechlich [tsair-br*e*k-lish]
France Frankreich [−rysh]
fraud der Betrug [buh-tr*oo*g]
free frei [fry]
   admission free Eintritt frei [ine−]
freeway die Autobahn [*őw*-toh-bahn]
frei (toilet) *vacant* (taxi) *free*
Freibad open-air pool
freight die Fracht [frah*k*t]
Fremdenzimmer rooms
French französisch [frants-*u*rr-zish]
   (person) Franzose [frants-oh-zuh]
   (woman) Französin [frantz-*u*rrs-zin]
french fries die Pomme frites [pom freet]
freshen up: I want to freshen up ich möchte
   mich frischmachen [ish m*u*rrshtuh mish
   fr*i*sh-mah*k*-en]
Friday Freitag [fry-tahg]

friend ein Freund [froynt]
friendly freundlich [froynt-lish]
from von [fon]
   from England aus England [ōwss eng-glannt]
   where is it from? wo kommt es her?
   [voh . . . ess hair]
front *(noun)* die Vorderseite [for-der-zy-tuh]
   in front of you vor Ihnen [for ee-nen]
   in the front vorn [forn]
frost der Frost
   frostbite die Frostbeule [−boy-luh]
frozen *(food)* tiefgekühlt [teef-gheh-kōolt]
   (person) eiskalt [ice−]
fruit das Obst [ohpst]
   fruit salad der Obstsalat [ohpst-zal-aht]
fry braten [brah-ten]
   nothing fried nichts Gebratenes [nix
   gheh-brah-ten-ess]
   fried egg ein Spiegelei [shpee-ghel-eye]
   frying pan die Bratpfanne [braht-pfann-uh]
full voll [foll]
fun: it's fun das macht Spaß [dass mahkt
shpass]
Fundbüro lost property
funny *(strange, comical)* komisch [koh−]
furniture die Möbel [murr-bel]
further weiter [vy−]
fuse die Sicherung [zisher-ŏong]
fuss das Theater [tay-ah-ter]
future die Zukunft [tsoo-kŏonft]
gale der Sturm [shtoorm]
gallon die Gallone [gal-oh-nuh]
» *TRAVEL TIP: 1 gallon = 3.8 liters*
gallstone ein Gallenstein [gal-en-shtine]
gamble spielen [shpee-len]; *(on horses)* wetten
[vet-en]
garage *(repair)* die Werkstatt [vairk-shtatt]
   (parking) die Garage [ga-rah-djuh]
garbage der Abfall [app-fal]
garden der Garten

garlic der Knoblauch [kuh-nohp-lōw*k*]
gas das Gas; *(car)* das Benzin [ben-tseen]
   gas cylinder der Gaszylinder [−tsōō-linnder]
   gas station die Tankstelle [−shtel-uh]
gasket die Dichtung [d*i*sh-tœng]
gay *(homosexual)* schwul [shvool]
gear der Gang
   (equipment) die Ausrüstung [ōws-rōōs-tœng]
   gearbox trouble Getriebeschaden
   [gheh-tree-buh-shah-den]
   gearshift der Schaltknüppel [−kuh-nōō-pel]
   (column-mounted) der Schalthebel [−hay-bel]
   I can't get it into gear ich kann den Gang
   nicht einlegen [ish kann dayn ... nisht
   ine-lay-ghen]
Gebühren charges
Gefahr danger
Gegenverkehr oncoming traffic
general delivery postlagernd [posst-lah-ghernt]
geöffnet open
Gepäckaufbewahrung left luggage
German deutsch [doytsh]; *(person)* Deutscher
   (woman) Deutsche [doytsh-uh]
   I don't speak German ich spreche kein
   Deutsch [ish shpresh-uh kine doytsh]
   the Germans die Deutschen
Germany Deutschland [d*o*ytsh-lannt]
geschlossen closed
Geschwindigkeitsbegrenzung speed limit
gesture eine Geste [gh*a*y-stuh]
get: will you get me a ... ? holen Sie mir bitte
   ein ... ? [hoh-len zee meer bittuh ine]
   how do I get to? wie komme ich zu ... ? [vee
   komm-uh ish tsoo]
   when can I get it back? wann bekomme ich
   es zurück? [van buh-komm-uh ish ess tsoo-rōōk]
   where do I get off? wo muß ich aussteigen?
   [voh mœss ish ōwss-shty-ghen]
   when do we get back? wann sind wir
   zurück? [van zinnt veer tsoo-rōōk]

where do I get a bus for...? wo fährt der Bus nach...? [voh fairt dair bœss nah*k*...app]
have you got...? haben Sie...? [h*a*h-ben zee]
will you come and get me? werden sie mich abholen? [vairden zie mich *a*pp-hoh-len]
gin ein Gin
  gin and tonic ein Gin Tonic
girl ein Mädchen [mayd-shen]
  my girlfriend meine Freundin [mine-uh froyn-din]
give geben [g*a*y-ben]
  I gave it to him ich habe es ihm gegeben [ish h*a*h-buh ess eem gheh-g*a*y-ben]
glad froh
glass das Glas
  a glass of water ein Glas Wasser [vasser]
glasses die Brille [brill-uh]
Gleis *platform*
gloves die Handschuhe [h*a*nnt-shoo-uh]
glue der Klebstoff [kl*a*yp-shtoff]
GmbH Gesellschaft mit beschränkter Haftung *Inc.*
go gehen [gay-en] *(by vehicle)* fahren
  where are you going? wo gehen Sie hin?
  my car won't go mein Auto fährt nicht [mine ōw-toh fairt nisht]
  when does the bus go? wann fährt der Bus? [vann fairt dair bœss]
  he's/it's gone er/es ist weg [air/ess isst vek]
goal das Tor
goat die Ziege [ts*ee*-guh]
God Gott
goggles *(ski)* die Schneebrille [shnay-brill-uh]
gold das Gold [gollt]
golf Golf
good gut [goot]
good-bye auf Wiedersehen [ōwf vee-duh-zayn]
gooseberries Stachelbeeren [sht*a*k-el-bay-ren]

grade crossing der Bahnübergang
  [bahn-ōōber-gang]
gram ein Gramm
» *TRAVEL TIP: 100 grams = approx 3½ oz*
grand großartig [grohss-arti*k*]
  my grandfather mein Großvater [–fah–]
  my grandmother meine Großmutter [–mōōt–]
  my grandson mein Enkel
  my granddaughter meine Enkelin
  [*e*ng-kel-inn]
grapefruit die Grapefruit
  grapefruit juice ein Grapefruitsaft [–zafft]
grapes Trauben [tró*w*-ben]
grass das Gras
grateful dankbar
  I'm very grateful to you ich bin Ihnen sehr
  dankbar [ish bin ee-nen zair . . .]
gratitude die Dankbarkeit [–kite]
gravy die Soße [*z*oh-suh]
gray grau [gró*w*]
grease das Fett; *(car, etc.)* die Wagenschmiere
  [v*a*h-ghen-shmee-ruh]
greasy fettig [–i*k*]
great groß; *(very good)* großartig [–arti*k*]
  great! klasse! [klass-uh]
greedy gierig [gh*ee*-ri*k*]
green grün [grōōn]
  greengrocer der Obst– und Gemüsehändler
  [ohbst oont gheh-mōō-zuh-hentler]
grocer's der Kaufmann [kó*w*f–]
ground der Boden [boh-den]
  on the ground auf dem Boden [ō*w*f daym . . .]
  on the ground floor im Erdgeschoß
  [. . . *a*irt-gheh-shoss]
group die Gruppe [grōōp-uh]
  our group leader der Leiter unserer Gruppe
  [l*y*-ter ōōn-zuh-ruh . . .]
  I'm with the American group ich gehöre zur
  amerikanischen Gruppe [ish gheh-h*u*rr-uh
  tsoor . . .]

guarantee die Garantie
  is there a guarantee? bekommen wir eine
  Garantie? [buh-kommen veer ine-un . . .]
guest der Gast
guesthouse die Pension [pen-zee-*ohn*]
guide der Führer [f*ōō*ruh]
guilty schuldig [sh*ō*l-di*k*]
guitar die Gitarre [ghee-*ta*-ruh]
gum *(in mouth)* der Gaumen [g*ōw*-men]
  (chewing) der Kaugummi [k*ōw*-goomee]
gun das Gewehr [gheh-v*air*]
  (pistol) die Pistole [−oh-luh]
gynecologist der Gynäkologe
  [g*ōō*-nay-koh-l*o*h-guh]
hair das Haar
  hairbrush die Haarbürste [−b*ōō*r-stuh]
  where can I get a haircut? wo kann ich mir
  die Haare schneiden lassen? [voh kann ish
  meer dee h*ah*-ruh shnyden lassen]
  is there a hairdresser's here? gibt es hier
  einen Friseur? [gheept ess heer ine-en
  free-z*ur*r]
» TRAVEL TIP: *hairdressers close on Mondays*
half halb [halp]
  a half portion eine halbe Portion [hal-buh
  portsee-*o*hn]
  half an hour eine halbe Stunde
  [. . . shtoon-duh]
halt stop
ham der Schinken
  hamburger ein Hamburger
hammer ein Hammer
hand die Hand [hannt]
  handbag die Handtasche [−tash-uh]
  handbrake die Handbremse [−brem-zuh]
handkerchief das Taschentuch [tash-en-too*k*]
handle der Griff
hand luggage das Handgepäck [−gheh-peck]
handmade handgearbeitet
  [h*a*nnt-gheh-ar-by-tet]
handsome gutaussehend [goot-*ō*ws-zay-ent]

hanger der Kleiderbügel
[kly-duh-b$\overline{oo}$-gel]
hangover der Kater [kahter]
my head is killing me mir platzt fast der
Kopf [meer...fasst dair...]
happen geschehen [gheh-shay-en]
I don't know how it happened ich weiß
nicht, wie es geschehen ist [ish vice nisht vee
ess...]
what's happening/happened? was ist los?
[vass isst lohs]
happy glücklich [gl$\overline{oo}$k-lish]
harbor der Hafen [hah-fen]
hard hart; *(difficult)* schwierig [shvee-ri$k$]
hard-boiled egg ein hartgekochtes Ei
[−gheh-ko$k$-tes eye]
push hard fest drücken [...dr$\overline{oo}$ken]
harm der Schaden [shah-den]
hat der Hut [hoot] *(knitted)* die Mütze [m$\overline{oo}$t-suh]
hate: I hate... ich hasse...[ish hass-uh]
have haben [hah-ben]
I have no time ich habe keine Zeit [ish
hah-buh kine-uh tsite]
do you have any cigars/a map? haben Sie
Zigarren/eine Karte? [hah-ben zee...]
can I have some water/some more? kann
ich etwas Wasser/noch ein bißchen haben?
[kann ish ett-vass vasser/no$k$ ine biss-shen
hah-ben]
I have to leave tomorrow ich muß morgen
abreisen [ish mooss mor-ghen $a$pp-ry-zen]
hayfever der Heuschnupfen [hoy-shn∞p-fen]
Hbf Hauptbahnhof central station
he er [air] **he is** er ist
head der Kopf
headache Kopfschmerzen [−schmair-tsen]
headlight der Scheinwerfer [shine-vairfer]
head waiter der Oberkellner [ohber−]
health die Gesundheit [gheh-z∞nt-hite]
your health! auf Ihr Wohl! [$\overline{o}$wf eer vohl]
healthy gesund [gheh-z∞nt]

hear: I can't hear ich höre nichts [ish hurr-uh nix]
   hearing aid das Hörgerät [hurr-gheh-rayt]
heart das Herz [hairts]
   heart attack ein Herzinfarkt
heat die Hitze [hit-suh]
   heat stroke ein Hitzschlag [hits-shlahg]
   heating die Heizung [hites-œng]
heavy schwer [shvair]
heel der Absatz [app-zats]
   could you put new heels on these? könnten Sie neue Absätze darauf machen? [kurrnten zee noy-uh app-zets-uh dah-rōwf mahken]
height die Höhe [hurr-uh]
   (person's) die Große [grurr-suh]
heiß hot
hello hallo
helmut der sturzhelm [shtœrts-helm]
help helfen
   can you help me? würden Sie mir helfen? [vœrden zee meer . . .]
   help! Hilfe! [hill-fuh]
her sie [zee]
   will you give it to her? würden Sie es ihr geben? [vœrden zee ess eer gay-ben]
   it's her bag, it's hers es ist ihre Tasche, es ist ihre [ess isst ee-ruh tash-uh]
here hier [heer]
   come here komm her! [. . . hair]
Herren men's room
high hoch [hohk]
highway die Autobahn [ōw-toh-bahn]
hill der Berg [bairk]
   up/down the hill den Berg hinauf/hinunter [dayn . . . hin-ōwf/hin-œnter]
him ihn [een]
   will you give it to him? würden Sie es ihm geben? [vœrden zee ess eem gay-ben]
   it's him er ist es [air isst ess]
his sein [zine]

it's his drink, it's his es ist sein Drink, es ist
seiner [ess isst zine-uh]
hit: he hit me er hat mich geschlagen [air hat
mish gheh-shlah-ghen]
hitchhike trampen [trempen]
  hitchhiker der Anhalter
Hochgarage *multi-storey parking lot*
Höchstgeschwindigkeit *maximum speed*
hold halten
hole das Loch [lok]
holiday der Feiertag
  I'm on holiday ich bin im Urlaub/in Ferien
Holland Holland [holl-annt]
home das Zuhause [tsoo-how-zuh]
  I want to go home ich möchte nach Hause
  [ish murrshtuh nahk how-zuh]
  at home zu Hause
  I'm homesick ich habe Heimweh [ish
  hah-buh hime-vay]
honest ehrlich [air-lish]
  honestly? ehrlich?
honey der Honig [hoh-nik]
honeymoon die Hochzeitsreise
  [hock-tsites-ry-zuh]
hood *(car)* die Motorhaube [−höwbuh]
hope die Hoffnung [hoff-noong]
  I hope that... ich hoffe, daß... [ish hoff-uh
  dass]
  I hope so/not hoffentlich/hoffentlich nicht!
  [hoff-ent-lish]
horizon der Horizont [horee-tsonnt]
horn *(car)* die Hupe [hoo-puh]
horrible schrecklich [−lish]
hors d'oeuvre das Hors d'oeuvre
horse das Pferd [pfairt]
hospital das Krankenhaus [−höws]
host der Gastgeber [−gay-ber]
hostess die Gastgeberin
hot heiß [hice] *(spiced)* scharf
hotel das Hotel

....

hotplate die Wärmplatte [vairm-plat-uh]
hot-water bottle die Wärmflasche [–flash-uh]
hour eine Stunde [shtoon-duh]
house das Haus [hōws]
   housewife eine Hausfrau [–frōw]
how wie [vee]
   how many wieviele [vee-feel-uh]
   how much wieviel [vee-feel]
   how often wie oft
   how long wie lange [. . . lang-uh]
   how long have you been here? seit wann
sind Sie da? [zite van zinnt zee dah]
   how are you? wie geht's? [vee gayts]
humid feucht [foysht]
humor der Humor [hoo-mor]
hungry hungrig [hoon-grik]
   I'm hungry/not hungry ich habe Hunger/ich
habe keinen Hunger [ish hah-buh
hoong-er/ . . . kine-en . . .]
hupen sound your horn
hurry: I'm in a hurry ich habe es eilig [ish
hah-buh ess eye-lik]
   please hurry! bitte beeilen Sie sich! [bittuh
buh-eye-len zee zish]
hurt: it hurts es tut weh [ess toot vay]
   my leg hurts mein Bein tut mir weh [mine
bine toot meer vay]
   YOU MAY HEAR...
ist es ein stechender Schmerz? [isst ess ine
shtek-ender shmairts] *is it a sharp pain?*
husband: my husband mein Mann [mine . . .]
I ich [ish]
   I am ich bin
ice das Eis [ice]
   ice pick der Eispickel
   ice cream das Eis
   iced coffee der Eiskaffee [–kaff-ay]
   with lots of ice mit viel Eis [mit feel . . .]
identity papers die Ausweispapiere
[ōws-vice-pap-ee-ruh]
idiot der Idiot [id-ee-oht]

if wenn [ven]
ignition die Zündung [tsōōn-doong]
ill krank; **I feel ill** ich fühle mich nicht wohl
[ish foo-luh mish nisht vohl]
illegal illegal [ill-ay-gahl]
illegible unleserlich [oon-lay-zair-lish]
illness die Krankheit [–hite]
Imbiß(stube) snack bar
immediately sofort [zohfort]
import der Import
important wichtig [vik-tik]
  it's very important es ist sehr wichtig [ess
  isst zair ...]
import duty der Einfuhrzoll [ine-foor-tsoll]
impossible unmöglich [oon-murr-glish]
impressive beeindruckend [buh-ine-drook-ent]
improve verbessern [fairbessern]
  I want to improve my German ich möchte
  besser Deutsch lernen [ish murrshtuh besser
  doytsh lair-nen]
in in
inch der Zoll [tsoll]
» *TRAVEL TIP: 1 inch = 2.54 cm*
include einschließen [ine-shlee-sen]
  does that include breakfast? ist Frühstück
  inbegriffen? [isst froo-shtook in-buh–]
inclusive inklusive [in-kloo-zee-vuh]
incompetent unfähig [oon-fay-ik]
inconsiderate unaufmerksam
  [oon-owf-mairk-zahm]
incredible unglaublich [oon-glowp-lish]
indecent unanständig [oo-an-shtendik]
independent unabhängig [oon-app-heng-ik]
India Indien [in-dee-un]
Indian indisch
  (person) Inder; *(woman)* Inderin
indicator der Blinker
indigestion die Magenverstimmung
  [mah-ghen-fair-shtim-oong]
indoors drinnen
industry die Industrie [in-doos-tree]

infection die Infektion [in-fekts-ee-*o*hn]
infectious ansteckend [*a*n-shteck-ent]
inflation die Inflation [in-flats-ee-*o*hn]
informal zwanglos [tsvang-lohs]; *(dress)* leger
[lay-j*a*ir]; *(agreement)* informell
information Informationen
[in-for-mats-ee-*o*h-nen]
  **do you have any information in English
  about...?** haben Sie Informationsmaterial in
  Englisch über...? [... –mah-tay-ree-ahl in
  eng-glish ōōber]
  is there an information office? gibt es da
  eine Informationsstelle? [gheept ess dah ine-uh
  –shtelluh]
inhabitant der Einwohner [*ine*-voh-nuh]
injection die Spritze [shprits-uh]
injured verletzt [fair-l*e*tst]
  he's been injured er ist verletzt
injury die Verletzung [fair-l*e*ts-ōong]
innocent unschuldig [ōon-sh*oo*l-di*k*]
insect ein Insekt [inzekt]
inside innen
insist: I insist (on it) ich bestehe darauf
[ish buh-sht*a*y-uh dah-r*o*wf]
insomnia die Schlaflosigkeit [shl*a*f-lohs-i*k*-kite]
instant coffee der Pulverkaffee [p*oo*l-ver-kaff-ay]
instead statt dessen [shtatt...]
  instead of anstelle von [an-sht*e*l-uh fon]
insulating tape das Isolierband
insulation die Isolierung [eez-oh-l*ee*rōong]
insult die Beleidigung [buh-l*i*de-ee-gōong]
insurance die Versicherung [fair-z*i*sh-erōong]
intelligent intelligent [–gh*e*nt]
interesting interessant [–*a*nt]
international international
[inter-nats-ee-oh-n*a*hl]
interpret: would you interpret for us? würden
Sie für uns dolmetschen? [v*ōō*rden zee f*ōō*r ōonts
d*o*ll-met-shen]
into in

introduce: can I introduce...? darf ich...
vorstellen? [... for-shtellen]
invalid *(noun)* der Kranke [–kuh]
(disabled) der Invalide [in-val-*ee*duh]
invitation die Einladung [*ine*-lah-d∞ng]
   thank you for the invitation danke für die
   Einladung [dankuh f∞r dee...]
invite: can I invite you out tonight? kann ich
Sie für heute abend einladen? [kan ish zee f∞r
hoytuh ah-bent *ine*-la-den]
invoice die Rechnung [resh-n∞ng]
Ireland Irland [*eer*-lannt]
Irish irisch [*eer*-ish]
   (person) Ire [*ee*ruh]; *(woman)* Irin [*ee*rin]
iron *(verb)* bügeln [b∞-geln]
   (noun) das Bügeleisen [–eye-zen]
   will you iron these for me? würden Sie diese
   für mich bügeln? [v∞rden zee deez-uh f∞r
   mish...]
is ist [isst]
island die Insel [*in*-zel]
it es [ess]
Italian italienisch [it-al-ee-*ay*-nish]
   (person) Italiener; *(woman)* Italienerin
Italy Italien [i-t*a*hl-ee-un]
itch ein Jucken [y∞cken]
   it itches es juckt [...y∞ckt]
itemize: would you itemize it for me? würden
Sie dies für mich aufschlüsseln? [v∞rden zee
dees f∞r mish *ó*wf-shl∞s-eln]
jack der Wagenheber [*vah*-ghen-hay-ber]
jacket die Jacke [yack-uh]
   (of man's suit) das Jackett
jam die Marmelade [mar-meh-l*a*h-duh]
   traffic jam der (Verkehrs)stau
   [fair-k*a*yrs-sht*ō*w]
January Januar [y*a*n-oo-ar]
jaw der Kiefer [k*ee*-fer]
jealous eifersüchtig [*eye*-fair-z∞k-tik]
jeans die Jeans

jellyfish die Qualle [kvalluh]
jetty der Pier
jewelry der Schmuck [schmoock]
job die Arbeit [ar-bite]
joke *(noun)* der Witz [vits]
    you must be joking das soll wohl ein Witz
    sein [dass zol vohl ine vits zine]
journey die Reise [ry-zuh]
July Juli [yoo-lee]
jumper cables ein Starthilfekabel
    [–hill-fuh-kah-bel]
junction die Kreuzung [kroy-tsoong]
June Juni [yoo-nee]
junk der Ramsch [ramsh]
just: just two nur zwei [noor tsvy]
    just a little nur ein wenig [. . . vayn-i*k*]
    just there genau dort [gheh-n*ow* . . .]
    that's just right das ist gerade richtig [dass
    isst gheh-r*a*h-duh ri*k*-ti*k*]
    not just now jetzt nicht [yets nisht]
    just now jetzt
    he was here just now er war gerade hier [air
    var gheh-r*a*h-duh heer]
kalt cold
Kasse cash register
keep: can I keep it? kann ich es behalten?
    [. . . buh-halten]
    you keep it Sie können es behalten [zee
    kurrnen . . .]
    keep the change der Rest ist für Sie
    [dair rest isst f*oo*r zee]
    you didn't keep your promise Sie haben Ihr
    Versprechen nicht gehalten [zee hah-ben eer
    fair-shpr*e*shen nisht gheh-halten]
    it keeps on breaking es geht dauernd kaputt
    [ess gayt d*ow*-ernt . . .]
kein Durchgang für Fußgänger no pedestrians
kein Trinkwasser not for drinking
kein Zutritt (für Unbefugte) no admittance (for
    unauthorized persons)
ketchup das (Tomaten)ketchup

kettle der Kessel
key der Schlüssel [shlōs-el]
kidney die Niere [nee-ruh]
kill töten [turr-ten]
kilo ein Kilo

» *TRAVEL TIP: conversion:* $\frac{kilos}{5} \times 11 = pounds$

kilos	1	1.5	5	6	7	8	9
pounds	2.2	3.3	11	13.2	15.4	17.6	19.8

kilometer ein Kilometer [–may-ter]

» *TRAVEL TIP: conversion:* $\frac{kilometers}{8} \times 5 = miles$

kilometers	1	5	10	20	50	100
miles		0.62	3.11	6.2	12.4	31	62

kind: that's very kind of you das ist sehr
  freundlich von Ihnen [. . . zair froynt-lish fon
  ee-nen]
  what kind of? was für ein? [vass fōr ine]
kiss der Kuß [kooss]
kitchen die Küche [kō-shuh]
knee das Knie [kuh-nee]
knife ein Messer
knock klopfen
  **there's a knocking noise from the
  engine** der Motor klopft
know wissen [vissen]
  (be acquainted with) kennen
  I don't know ich weiß nicht [ish vice
  nisht]
  I know him ich kenne ihn [. . . ken-uh een]
Krankenhaus hospital
Kreuzung crossroads
kurvenreiche Strecke bends
label das Etikett
laces *(shoe)* Schnürsenkel [shnōr-zenkel]
lacquer der Lack
lady eine Dame [dah-muh]
lager ein helles Bier [. . . beer]
lake der See [zay]
lamb *(meat)* das Lamm
lamp die Lampe [lamp-uh]

lampshade der Lampenschirm [–sheerm]
lamppost der Laternenpfahl
[lah-*t*airn-en-pfahl]
land *(noun)* das Land [lannt]
lane *(car)* die Spur [spoor]
langsam fahren *drive slowly*
language die Sprache [shpr*ah-k*uh]
large groß [grohss]
laryngitis die Kehlkopfentzündung
[k*a*yhl-kopf-en-ts$\overline{oo}$n-d∞ng]
last letzter [lets-ter]
    last year/week letztes Jahr/letzte Woche
    last night gestern abend; *(late)* gestern nacht
    [ghestern ah-bent/nah*k*t]
    at last! endlich! [ent-lish]
late: sorry I'm late entschuldigen Sie, daß ich
    zu spät komme [ent-sh∞l-dig-en zee dass ish
    tsoo shpayt kommuh]
    it's a bit late es ist ein bißchen spät
    [. . . bis-shen . . .]
    please hurry, I'm late bitte beeilen Sie sich,
    ich bin spät dran [bittuh buh-eye-len zee zish
    ish bin shpayt dran]
    at the latest spätestens [shpayt-es-tenz]
    later später [shpayter]
    I'll come back later ich komme später
    zurück
    see you later! bis später!
laugh *(verb)* lachen [lah-*k*en]
launderette die Münzwäscherei
[m$\overline{oo}$nts-vesh-er-eye]
» *TRAVEL TIP: not very many of these in Germany;*
   try a "Sofortreinigung"
laundry detergent des Waschpulver [–p∞lver]
law das Gesetz [gheh-zets]
Lawinengefahr *danger of avalanches*
lawyer der Rechtsanwalt [reshts-anvalt]
laxative ein Abführmittel [app-f$\overline{oo}$r-mittel]
lazy faul [f$\overline{o}$wl]
leaf das Blatt

leak eine undichte Stelle [oon-dish-tuh shtel-uh]
  it leaks es ist nicht dicht
learn: I want to learn ich möchte ... lernen [ish
  murrshtuh ... lair-nen]
lease *(verb)* mieten [meeten]
  (land, business premises) pachten [pak-ten]
least: not in the least nicht im geringsten
  [nisht im gheringsten]
  at least mindestens [minn-dess-tenz]
leather das Leder [lay-der]
  the meat's like leather dieses Fleisch ist zäh
  wie Leder [deez-es flysh isst tsay vee lay-der]
leave: we're leaving tomorrow wir fahren
  morgen ab [veer fah-ren ... app]
  when does the bus leave? wann fährt der
  Bus? [van fairt dair booss]
  I left two shirts in my room ich habe zwei
  Hemden in meinem Zimmer liegenlassen [ish
  hah-buh tsvy ... lee-ghen-lassen]
  can I leave this here? kann ich das
  hierlassen? [... heerlassen]
Lebensgefahr *danger*
left linke; **on the left** links
  to be left-handed Linkshänder sein
  [links-hender zine]
left luggage (office) die Gepäckaufbewahrung
  [gheh-peck-ōwf-buh-vah-roong]
leg das Bein [bine]
legal legal [lay-gahl]
  legal aid die Rechtshilfe [reshts-hil-fuh]
lemon die Zitrone [tsi-troh-nuh]
lemonade eine Limonade [lee-moh-na-duh]
lend: will you lend me your ... ? leihen Sie
  mir Ihr ... ? [lye-en zee meer eer ...]
lengthen verlängern [fair-lengern]
  (clothes) länger machen [lenger mah-ken]
lens *(of glasses)* das Glas [glahss]
  (camera) das Objektiv [opp-yek-teef]
Lent die Fastenzeit [fass-ten-tsite]
less weniger [vay-nee-gher]

let: let me help darf ich Ihnen helfen?
[. . . ee-nen . . .]
   let me go! lassen Sie mich los! [. . . lohs]
   will you let me off here? würden Sie mich
hier aussteigen lassen [vōōrden zee mish heer
ōōws-shty-ghen . . .]
   let's go gehen wir! [gay-en veer]
letter der Brief [breef]
   are there any letters for me? habe ich Post?
[hah-buh ish posst]
   letterbox der Briefkasten [breefkasten]
lettuce ein Kopfsalat [kopf-za-laht]
liable *(responsible)* haftbar
library die Bibliothek [bee-blee-oh-tayk]
license die Genehmigung [gheh-nay-mee-goong]
   license plate das Nummernschild
[noomern-shillt]
lid der Deckel
lie *(noun)* eine Lüge [lōō-guh]
   can he lie down for a bit? kann er sich ein
bißchen hinlegen? [kan air zish ine bis-shen
hin-lay-ghen]
life das Leben [lay-ben]
   life insurance die Lebensversicherung
[lay-benz-fair-zish-er-oong]
   not at my time of life! nicht in meinem Alter!
[nischt in mine-em al-ter]
   lifeboat das Rettungsboot [−boht]
   lifeguard der Bademeister [bah-duh-my-ster]
(on beach) der Rettungsschwimmer
[−shvimmer]
   life jacket eine Schwimmweste [schvim-vest-uh]
lift: do you want a lift? kann ich Sie
mitnehmen? [kan ish zee mit-nay-men]
   could you give me a lift? könnten Sie mich
mitnehmen? [kurrnten . . .]
light *(noun)* das Licht [lisht]
(adjective) leicht [lysht]
   the lights aren't working das Licht geht
nicht [. . . gayt nisht]

(car) die Scheinwerfer funktionieren nicht
[shine-vairfer fōonk-tsee-ohn-ee-ren ...]
have you got a light? haben Sie Feuer?
[hah-ben zee foy-er]
when it gets light wenn es hell wird
[ven ... virt]
   light bulb die Glühbirne [glōō-beer-nuh]
   the bulb's gone out die Birne ist
durchgebrannt [... ist dōorsh-gheh-brannt]
   light meter der Belichtungsmesser
[buh-lish-tōongs-messer]
like: would you like ...? möchten Sie ...?
[murrshten zee]
   I'd like a .../I'd like to ... ich hätte gerne
ein .../ich würde gerne ... [ish hett-uh
gairn-uh ine/vōorduh ...]
   I like it/you das gefällt mir/ich mag Sie gern
[dass gheh-felt meer/ish mahg zee gairn]
   I don't like it das gefällt mir nicht [gheh-felt
meer nisht]
   like this one wie dieser [vee dee-zer]
   what's it like? wie ist es? [vee ...]
   do it like this machen Sie es so [mah-ken zee
ess zoh]
lime die Limone [lee-moh-nuh]
line die Linie [lee-nee-uh] *(for tickets, etc.)* die
Schlange [shlang-uh]
lip die Lippe [lip-uh]
   lipstick der Lippenstift [−shtift]
liqueur ein Likör [lik-urr]
list *(noun)* die Liste [list-uh]
listen zuhören [tsoo-hurr-ren]
   listen! hören Sie zu! [hurr-ren zee tsoo]
liter der Liter [lee-ter]
» *TRAVEL TIP: 1 liter = 1.06 pints = 0.26 gals*
little klein [kline]
   a little ice/a little more ein wenig Eis/noch
ein wenig [ine vay-nik ice/nok ...]
   just a little nur ein wenig, nur ein bißchen
[noor ... bis-shen]

live leben [lay-ben]
    I live in... ich wohne in [ish voh-nuh...]
    where do you live? wo wohnen Sie? [voh voh-nen zee]
liver die Leber [lay-ber]
LKW = Lastkraftwagen truck
loaf ein Brot [broht]
lobster ein Hummer [hoommer]
local: could we try a local wine? können wir einen Wein aus der Gegend probieren? [kurrnen veer ine-en vine öwss dair gay-ghent proh-bee-ren]
    a local restaurant ein Restaurant im Ort [... res-tor-rong...]
    is it made locally? wird es hier hergestellt? [virt ess heer hair-gheh-shtelt]
lock: the lock's broken das Schloß ist kaputt [... shloss...]
    I've locked myself out ich habe mich ausgeschlossen [ish hah-buh mish öwss-gheh-shlossen]
lonely einsam [ine-zahm]
long lang
    we'd like to stay longer wir würden gerne etwas länger bleiben [veer vöörden gairn-uh etvass leng-er bly-ben]
    that was long ago das ist lange her [... lang-uh hair]
look: you look tired Sie sehen müde aus [zee zay-en möö-duh öwss]
    I'm looking forward to... ich freue mich auf... [ish froy-uh mish öwf]
    I'm looking for... ich suche... [ish zook-uh]
    I'm just looking ich möchte mich nur umschauen [ish murrsh-tuh mish noor oom-shöw-en]
    look at that schauen Sie sich das an! [shöw-en zee zish dass an]
    look out! Vorsicht! [for-zisht]
loose lose [loh-zuh]
lose verlieren [fair-lee-ren]

I've lost my... ich habe mein... verloren
[ish hah-buh mine... fair-lor-ren]
  excuse me, I'm lost entschuldigen Sie, ich
  habe mich verlaufen [ent-shool-dig-en zee ish
  hah-buh mish fair-lŏwf-en]
  (driving) ich habe mich verfahren
  [... fair-fah-ren]
  lost and found office das Fundbüro
  [fŏont-bōō-roh]
lot: a lot/not a lot viel/nicht viel [feel]
  a lot of french fries/wine eine Menge
  Pommes Frites/Wein [ine-uh meng-uh pom
  freet/vine]
  lots of jede Menge [yay-duh...]
  a lot more expensive viel teurer [feel toy-rer]
lotion die Lotion [lohts-ee-ohn]
loud laut [lŏwt]; **louder** lauter [lŏwter]
love: I love you ich liebe dich [ish lee-buh dish]
  he's in love er ist verliebt [air isst fair-leept]
  I love this wine ich mag diesen Wein sehr
  gern [ish mahg dee-zen vine zair gairn]
  do you love me? liebst du mich? [leepst doo
  mish]
lovely schön [shurrn]
low niedrig [nee-drik]
  low beams Abblendlicht [app-blent-lisht]
luck das Glück [glōock]
  good luck! viel Glück! [feel glōock]
lucky Glücks– [glōocks–]
  you're lucky Sie haben Glück [zee hah-ben
  glōock]
  that's lucky das ist Glück [dass isst...]
luggage das Gepäck [gheh-peck]
lumbago der Hexenschuß [hexen-shŏoss]
lump die Beule [boy-luh]
  (inside) die Geschwulst [gheh-shvŏolst]
lunch das Mittagessen [mi-tahg-essen]
lung die Lunge [lŏong-uh]
Luxembourg Luxemburg [lŏoxembŏorg]
luxurious luxuriös [lŏox-oo-ree-urrs]
luxury der Luxus [lŏox-ŏoss]

machine die Maschine [mash-ee-nuh]
mad verrückt [fair-rōockt]
madam gnädige Frau [guh-nay-dig-uh frōw]
made-to-measure nach Maß [nah*k* mahss]
magazine die Zeitschrift [tsite-shrift]
magnificent großartig [grohss-ahr-ti*k*]
maid das Zimmermädchen [ts*i*mmer-mayd-shen]
maiden name der Mädchenname
  [maid-shen-nah-muh]
mail die Post [posst]; **is there any mail for
  me?** habe ich Post? [h*a*h-buh ish . . .]
  mailbox der Briefkasten
» *TRAVEL TIP: mailboxes are yellow*
main road die Hauptstraße [hōwpt-shtrahss-uh]
make machen [mah-*k*en]
  will we make it in time? schaffen wir das
  rechtzeitig? [shaffen veer dass resht-tsyti*k*]
makeup das Make-up
man der Mann
manager der Geschäftsführer
  [gheh-sh*e*fts-fōor-er]
  can I see the manager? kann ich mit dem
  Geschäftsführer sprechen? [. . . shpreshen]
manicure die Maniküre [man-ee-kōo-ruh]
manners die Manieren [man-*ee*-ren]
many viele [feel-uh]
map die Karte [kar-tuh]; **a map of . . .** eine
  Karte von . . . [ine-uh kar-tuh fon]
March März [mairts]
margarine die Margarine [mar-ga-r*ee*n-uh]
marina der Jachthafen [ya*k*t-hah-fen]
mark: there's a mark on it es ist beschädigt
  [. . . buh-sh*a*y-di*k*t]
  (stained) da ist ein Fleck darauf [dah-rōwf]
market der Markt
  marketplace der Marktplatz
marmalade die Orangenmarmelade
  [or*o*n-djen-mar-meh-lah-duh]
married verheiratet [fair-hy-raht-et]
marry: will you marry me? willst du mich
  heiraten? [villst doo mish hy-rahten]

marvelous wunderbar [voonderbar]
mascara die Wimperntusche [vimpern-toosh-uh]
mashed potatoes der Kartoffelbrei
  [kartoffel-bry]
massage eine Massage [massah-djuh]
mast der Mast [masst]
mat die Matte [mat-uh]
match: a box of matches eine Schachtel
  Streichhölzer [sha*k*-tel shtrysh-hurltser]
  soccer match ein Fußballspiel
  [fooss-bal-shpeel]
material das Material [ma-tay-ree-*a*hl]
matter: it doesn't matter das macht nichts
  [dass mah*k*t nix]
  what's the matter? was ist los? [vass isst
  lohs]
mattress die Matratze [ma-tr*a*ts-uh]
mature reif [rife]
maximum maximal [maxi-mahl]
  (noun) das Maximum [maximoom]
  that's our maximum offer das ist unser
  höchstes Angebot [. . . oonz-er hurrk-stess
  an-gheh-boht]
May Mai [my]
may: may I have . . . ? darf ich . . . haben?
  [. . . ish . . . h*a*h-ben]
maybe vielleicht [fee-lysht]
mayonnaise die Mayonnaise [my-on-ay-zuh]
me mich [mish]
  with/from me mit/von mir [. . . fon meer]
  give it to me geben Sie es mir
  it was me ich war es [ish var ess]
meal das Essen
mean: what does this mean? was heißt das?
  [vass hysst dass]
  by all means! aber natürlich [ah-ber
  natoor-lish]
measles die Masern [m*a*h-zern]
  German measles die Röteln [rurr-teln]
measurements die Maße [mahss-uh]
meat das Fleisch [flysh]

mechanic: is there a mechanic here? gibt es
hier einen Mechaniker? [gheept ess heer ine-en
meck-*ah*hn-iker]

medicine die Medizin [medi-ts*ee*n]

meet treffen

pleased to meet you angenehm!
[*a*n-gheh-naym]

meeting die Besprechung [buh-shpresh-∞ng]
(conference) die Sitzung [zits∞ng]

melon eine Melone [meh-l*o*h-nuh]

member das Mitglied [mit-gleet]

how do I become a member? wie werde ich
Mitglied? [vee vair-duh ish mit-gleet]

men die Männer [men-er]

mend: can you mend this? können Sie dies
flicken? [kurrnen zee dees . . .]

mention: don't mention it gern geschehen
[gairn gheh-sh*a*y-en]

menu die Speisekarte [shpy-zuh-kar-tuh]

can I have the menu, please? kann ich,
bitte, die Speisekarte haben?

merge *(traffic)* die Abbiegerspur
[*a*pp-bee-gher-spoor]

mess die Durcheinander [d∞rsh-ine-ander]

message: are there any messages for me? hat
jemand eine Nachricht für mich hinterlassen?
[. . . yay-mannt ine-uh nah*k*-risht f∞r mish . . .]

can I leave a message for . . . ? kann ich eine
Nachricht für . . . hinterlassen?

meter der Meter [may-ter]

» *TRAVEL TIP: 1 meter = 39.37 ins = 1.09 yds*

midday der Mittag [mi-tahg]

middle die Mitte [mittuh]

in the middle in der Mitte [in dair mittuh]

midnight Mitternacht [mitter-nah*k*t]

might: I might be wrong vielleicht hab' ich
unrecht [fee-lysht hahb ish ∞n-resht]

he might have gone er ist vielleicht schon
gegangen [air isst fee-lysht shohn
gheh-gang-en]

migraine die Migräne [mee-grain-uh]
mild mild [milt]
mile die Meile [my-luh]
» TRAVEL TIP: conversion: $\frac{miles}{5} \times 8 = kilometers$

miles	.5	1	3	5	10	50	100
kilometers	0.8	1.6	4.8	8	16	80	160

milk die Milch [milsh]
  a glass of milk ein Glas Milch
  milkshake das Milchmixgetränk
  [milsh-mix-gheh-trenk]
millimeter der Millimeter [–mayter]
minced meat das Hackfleisch [hack-flysh]
mind: I've changed my mind ich habe es mir
  anders überlegt [ish hah-buh ess meer anders
  ōberlaygt]
  I don't mind das macht mir nichts aus
  [dass mahkt meer nix ōwss]
  do you mind if I...? macht es Ihnen etwas
  aus, wenn ich...? [mahkt ess ee-nen et-vass
  ōwss ven ish...]
  never mind macht nichts [mahkt nix]
mine mein [mine]
mineral water das Mineralwasser
  [minerahl-vasser]
minimum das Minimum [minimoom]
minus minus [mee-nooss]
minute die Minute [minoo-tuh]
  he'll be here in a minute er kommt gleich
  [air...glysh]
  just a minute einen Moment, bitte [ine-en
  moh-ment bittuh]
mirror der Spiegel [shpee-ghel]
Miss Fräulein [froy-line]
miss: I miss you du fehlst mir [doo faylst meer]
  he's missing er ist verschwunden [air isst
  fair-shvoonden]
  there's a...missing da fehlt ein... [dah
  faylt ine...]
mist der Nebel [naybel]

Vorspeisen Hors d'oeuvre
Geräucherter Aal *smoked eel*
Königspastete *chicken vol-au-vent*
Krabbencocktail *crab cocktail*
Meefischli *small fried fish from River Main*
Weinbergschnecken *snails*

Suppen Soups
Blumenkohlsuppe *cream of cauliflower*
Brotsuppe *(Black Forest) bread soup*
Flädlesuppe *(Swabia) consommé with pancake
    strips*
Hühnerbrühe *chicken broth*
Klößchensuppe *clear soup with dumplings*
Kraftbrühe mit Ei *consommé with a raw egg*
Ochsenschwanzsuppe *oxtail soup*
Tagessuppe *soup of the day*

Vom Rind Beef
Bouletten *(Berlin) meat balls*
Deutsches Beefsteak *mince patty*
Rinderbraten *pot roast*
Rinderfilet *fillet steak*
Rindsrouladen *stuffed beef rolls*
Rostbraten *(Swabia) steak with onions*
Sauerbraten *marinaded pot roast*

Vom Schwein Pork
Eisbein *knuckles of pork*
Karbonade *(Berlin) roast ribs of pork*
Kotelett *chops*
Leberkäse *(South Germany) baked pork and
    beef loaf*
Schweinebraten *roast pork*
Schweineschnitzel *pork fillets*

Vom Kalb Veal
Gefüllte Kalbsbrust *veal roll*
Kalbshaxe *leg of veal*
Jägerschnitzel *veal with mushrooms*
Wienerschnitzel *veal in breadcrumbs*
Zigeunerschnitzel *veal with peppers and relishes*

Wild Game
Rehbraten *roast venison*
Wildschweinsteak *wild boar steak*

Fischgerichte Fish
Forelle Müllerin *trout with butter and lemon*
Hecht *pike*
Karpfen blau *boiled blue carp*
Matjesheringe *pickled herrings*

Other Meats
Bockwurst *large Frankfurter sausage*
Bratwurst *grilled pork sausage*
Halbes Hähnchen *half a (roast) chicken*

Spezialitäten Specialties
Himmel und Erde *(Rhineland) potatoes and
    apple sauce with black pudding*
Kohl und Pinkel *(Bremen) cabbage and potatoes
    with sausages and smoked meat*
Labskaus *(Hamburg) potatoes mixed with pieces
    of fish and meat*
Weißwürste mit Senf *(Munich) white sausages
    and sweet mustard*

Beilagen Side dishes
Blumenkohl *cauliflower;* Bratkartoffeln *roast
    potatoes;* Erbsen *peas;* gemischter Salat
    mixed salad; Gemüseplatte *mixed vegetables;*
    Kartoffelpüree *mashed potatoes;* Klöße,
    Knödel *dumplings;* Pommes Frites
    French fried potatoes; Rosenkohl
    Brussel sprouts; Salzkartoffel *boiled
    potatoes;* Sauerkraut *finely chopped
    pickled cabbage;* Spargel *asparagus;*
    Spätzle *homemade noodles*

Nachspeisen Desserts
Gemischtes Eis mit Sahne *assorted ice creams
    with whipped cream*
Obstsalat *fruit salad*
Rote Grütze *(North Germany) fruit blancmange*

mistake ein Fehler [fayler]
   I think you've made a mistake ich glaube,
   Sie haben sich vertan [ish glōw-buh zee
   hah-ben zish fair-tan]
misunderstanding ein Mißverständnis
   [miss-fair-shtent-niss]
modern modern [modairn]
Monday Montag [mohntahg]
money das Geld [gelt]
   I've lost my money ich habe mein Geld
   verloren [ish hah-buh mine gelt fair-lor-ren]
   no money kein Geld [kine gelt]
   they've taken all my money man hat mir
   mein ganzes Geld gestohlen [. . . meer mine
   gants-es gelt gheh-shtohlen]
month der Monat [moh-naht]
moon der Mond [mohnt]
moped das Moped
more mehr [mair]
   can I have some more? kann ich noch etwas
   haben? [kan ish nok et-vass hah-ben]
   more wine, please noch ein wenig Wein,
   bitte [nok ine vaynik vine bittuh]
   no more nicht mehr [nisht mair]
   more comfortable bequemer [buh-kvay-mer]
   more than mehr als [mair-alz]
morning der Morgen [mor-ghen]
   this morning heute morgen [hoy-tuh . . .]
   good morning guten Morgen [gooten . . .]
   in the morning morgens [morghenz]
most: I like it/you most das gefällt/Sie gefallen
   mir am besten [. . . gheh-fellt/zee gheh-fal-en
   meer . . .]
   most of the time/most of the people
   meistens/die meisten Leute [my-stenz/dee
   my-sten loy-tuh]
mother: my mother meine Mutter [mine-uh
   mooter]
motor der Motor
motorbike das Motorrad [−raht]
motorboat das Motorboot [−boht]

motorcyclist der Motorradfahrer
  [mot*o*r-raht-fah-rer]
motorhome der Wohnwagen [vohn-vah-ghen]
mountain der Berg [bairk]
  mountaineer ein Bergsteiger [–shtyger]
  mountaineering das Bergsteigen [–shtygen]
mouse die Maus [mōwss]
moustache der Schnurrbart [schnoor-bahrt]
mouth der Mund [moont]
move: don't move bewegen Sie sich nicht!
  [buh-vay-ghen zee zish nisht]
  could you move your car? könnten Sie
  Ihren Wagen wegfahren? [kurrnten zee ee-ren
  vah-ghen vek-fahren]
movie ein Film
  let's go to the movies gehen wir ins kino
  [gay-en veer ints kee-noh]
  movie theater das kino [kee-noh]
Mr. Herr [hair]
Mrs. Frau [frōw]
Ms Frau [frōw]
much viel [feel]
  much better/much more viel besser/viel
  mehr [feel . . . /feel mair]
  not much nicht viel [nisht feel]
muffler *(car)* der Schalldämpfer [sh*a*ll-dem-pfer]
mug: I've been mugged ich bin überfallen
  worden [ish bin ōber-fal-en vorden]
mom: my mom meine Mutti [moo-tee]
muscle der Muskel [m*oo*ss-kel]
museum das Museum [moo-zay-oom]
mushroom der Pilz [pilts]
music die Musik [moozeek]
must: I must ich muß [ish m*oo*ss]
  I must not eat . . . ich darf . . . nicht essen
  [ish darf . . . nisht . . .]
  you must do it Sie müssen es tun [zee
  mōssen ess toon]
mustard der Senf [zenf]
MWSt = Mehrwertsteuer sales tax
my mein [mine]

nail *(finger, wood)* der Nagel [nah-ghel]
  nailfile die Nagelfeile [−fy-luh]
  nail polish der Nagellack [−lack]
  nail clippers der Nagelzwicker [−tsvicker]
  nail scissors die Nagelschere [−shay-ruh]
naked nackt
name der Name [nah-muh]
  first name der Vorname [for-nah-muh]
  my name is... ich heiße... [ish hyss-uh...]
  what's your name? wie heißen Sie? [vee
  hyssen zee]
napkin *(paper)* die Serviette [zair-vee-ettuh]
narrow eng
national national [nats-ee-oh-nahl]
nationality die Nationalität
  [nats-ee-oh-nahl-ee-tayt]
natural natürlich [natōrlish]
naughty: don't be naughty sei nicht frech
  [zy nisht fresh]
near: is it near? ist es in der Nähe? [isst ess in
  dair nay-uh]
  near here hier herum [heer hairoom]
  do you go near...? kommen Sie in die Nähe
  von...? [...zee in dee nay-uh fon]
  where's the nearest...? wo ist der (die/das)
  nächste...? [voh ist dair (dee/dass) nex-tuh]
nearly fast [fasst]
neat *(drink)* pur [poor]
necessary notwendig [noht-vendik]
  it's not necessary das ist nicht notwendig
neck der Hals [halz]
  necklace das Halsband [halz-bannt]
need: I need a... ich brauche einen... [ish
  browk-uh ine-en...]
needle die Nadel [nah-del]
negotiations die Verhandlungen
  [fair-hannt-loong-en]
neighbor der Nachbar [nahk-bar]
neither: neither of them keiner von beiden
  [kine-er fon by-den]

neither ... nor ... weder ... noch ...
[vayder ... no*k* ...]
neither do I ich auch nicht [ish ōw*k* nisht]
nephew: my nephew mein Neffe [mine neffuh]
nervous nervös [nair-vurrs]
net das Netz
net price der Nettopreis [–price]
never niemals [n*ee*-malz]
new neu [noy]
news die Nachrichten [nah*k*-rishten]
newsstand der Zeitungshändler
[tsyt**œ**ngs-henntler]
newspaper die Zeitung [tsyt**œ**ng]
do you have any English newspapers?
haben Sie englische Zeitungen? [hah-ben zee
eng-glish-uh tsyt**œ**ng-en]
New Year Neujahr [noy-yahr]
New Year's Eve Silvester
Happy New Year! ein gutes neues Jahr! [ine
gootes noy-es yahr]
» *TRAVEL TIP: New Year is celebrated with
fireworks and traditionally champagne at
midnight when people say "Prosit Neujahr"*
[prohst noy-yahr]; *the next day and afterwards
they say "ein gutes neues Jahr"*
New Zealand Neuseeland [noy-zay-lannt]
New Zealander Neuseeländer [–lender]
(woman) Neuseeländerin
next nächster [nexter]
please stop at the next corner halten Sie,
bitte, an der nächsten Ecke [... zee bittuh an
dair nexten eckuh]
see you next year bis nächstes Jahr [bis
nextes yahr]
sit next to me setzen Sie sich neben mich
[zet-sen zee zish nay-ben mish]
nice schön [shurrn] *(person)* nett
nicht berühren *do not touch*
nicht öffnen *do not open*
Nichtraucher *no smoking*

niece: my niece meine Nichte [mine-uh nishtuh]

night die Nacht [nah*k*t]

  good night gute Nacht [gootuh nah*k*t]

  at night nachts [nah*k*ts]

  where's a good nightclub? wo ist ein guter Nachtklub [voh isst ine gooter nah*k*t-klɷb]

  nightlife das Nachtleben [nah*k*t-lay-ben]

  night porter der Nachtportier [nah*k*t-por-tee-ay]

no nein [nine]

  there's no water wir haben kein Wasser [veer h*a*h-ben kine vasser]

  no way! auf keinen Fall! [ōwf kine-en fal]

nobody neimand [nee-mannt]

  nobody saw it keiner hat es gesehen [kine-er hat ess gheh-z*a*y-en]

noisy laut [lōwt]

  our room's too noisy in unserem Zimmer ist es zu laut [in ɷnzerem tsimmer isst ess tsoo . . .]

none keiner [kine-er]; **none of them** keiner von ihnen [kine-er fon ee-nen]

nonsense Quatsch [kvatsh]

normal normal [norm*a*hl]

north der Norden

Northern Ireland Nordirland [nort-*ee*r-lannt]

nose die Nase [nah-zuh]

nosebleed das Nasenbluten [nah-zen-bloo-ten]

not nicht [nisht]

  I'm not hungry ich habe keinen Hunger [ish h*a*h-buh kine-en hɷng-er]

  not that one das nicht [dass nisht]

  not me ich nicht

  I don't understand ich verstehe das nicht [ish fair-sht*a*y-uh dass nisht]

  he didn't tell me er hat mir das nicht gesagt [air hat meer dass nisht gheh-zahgt]

Notausgang emergency exit

Notbremse emergency brake

nothing nichts [nix]
November November
now jetzt [yetst]
nowhere nirgends [neer-ghenz]
nudist der FKK-Anhänger [eff-ka-ka-an-heng-er]
  nudist beach der FKK-Strand [−shtrannt]
nuisance: it's a nuisance das ist ärgerlich [dass
  isst air-guh-lish]
  this man's being a nuisance der Mann
  belästigt mich [. . . buh-lest-ikt mish]
numb taub [tōwp]
number die Zahl [tsahl]
nurse die Krankenschwester [kranken-shvester]
  (male) der Pfleger [pflay-gher]
nut die Nuß [nœss]
  (for bolt) die (Schrauben)mutter
  [shrōwben-mœoter]
oar das Ruder [rooder]
obligatory obligatorisch [oh-bleegator-rish]
obviously offensichtlich [off-en-zisht-lish]
occasionally gelegentlich [gheh-lay-ghent-lish]
occupied besetzt [buh-zetst]
  is this seat occupied? sitzt hier jemand?
  [zitst heer yay-mannt]
o'clock *see* **time**
October Oktober
odd *(number)* ungerade [œn-gheh-rah-duh]
  (strange) seltsam [zelt-zahm]
of von [fon]
off: it just came off es ist einfach abgegangen
  [. . . ine-fahk app-gheh-gang-en]
  10% off 10% Ermäßigung [tsayn proh-tsent
  air-mace-ee-gœng]
office das Büro [bōroh]
official *(noun)* der Beamte [buh-am-tuh]
Öffnungszeiten *opening hours*
often oft
oil das Öl [urrl]
  I'm losing oil mein Wagen verliert Öl [mine
  vah-ghen fair-leert urrl]

will you change the oil? könnten Sie, bitte, das Öl wechseln? [kurrnten zee bittuh dass urrl vek-seln]

ointment die Salbe [zahl-buh]

OK okay

old alt; **how old are you?** wie alt sind Sie? [vee alt zinnt zee]

olive die Olive [oh-*lee*-vuh]

omelette ein Omelett(e) [omuh-lett(uh)]

on auf [ōwf]

  I haven't got it on me ich habe es nicht bei mir [ish hah-buh ess nisht by meer]

  on Friday am Freitag [am fry-tahg]

  on television im Fernsehen [im fairn-zay-en]

once einmal [ine-mahl]

  at once sofort [zoh-fort]

one ein [ine] *(number)* eins [ine-ts]

  the red one der [die/das] rote [dair (dee/dass) roh-tuh]

one-way ticket/two one-way tickets

  to . . . einmal einfach/zweimal einfach nach . . . [ine-mal ine-fah*k*/tsvy-mal ine-fah*k* nah*k*]

onion die Zwiebel [tsvee-bel]

only nur [noor]

  he is the only one er ist der einzige [air isst dair ine-tsig-uh]

open *(adjective)* offen

  (shop) geöffnet [gheh-urrf-net]

  I can't open it ich bekomme es nicht auf [ish buh-kommuh ess nisht ōwf]

  when do you open? wann machen Sie auf? [van mah*k*en zee ōwf]

opera die Oper [oh-per]

operation die Operation [oh-per-ats-ee-*o*hn]

  will I need an operation? muß ich operiert werden? [mooss ish oh-per-*ee*rt vairden]

operator *(tel)* die Vermittlung [fair-m*i*tt-loong]

opposite: opposite the hotel gegenüber dem Hotel [gay-ghen-oober daym . . .]

optician der Optiker

or oder [oh-der]
orange die Orange [oronj-uh]
  orange juice der Orangensaft [oronjen-zafft]
order: could we order now? könnten wir jetzt
  bestellen? [kurrnten veer yetst buh-shtellen]
  thank you, we've already ordered danke,
  wir haben schon bestellt [dankuh veer hah-ben
  shohn buh-shtellt]
other: the other one der (die, das) andere [dair
  (dee, dass) an-der-uh]
  do you have any others? haben Sie
  irgendwelche anderen? [hah-ben zee
  irgent-velsh-uh an-der-en]
otherwise sonst
ought: I ought to go ich sollte gehen [ish
  zolltuh gay-en]
ounce die Unze [oonts-uh]
» *TRAVEL TIP: 1 ounce = 28.35 grams*
our unser [oon-zer]
  that's ours das ist unseres [. . . oon-zer-es]
out: we're out of gas uns ist das Benzin
  ausgegangen [oonz isst dass ben-tseen
  ōwss-gheh-gang-en]
  get out! raus! [rōwss]
outdoors im Freien [im fry-en]
outlet *(electrical)* die Steckdose [shteck-doh-zuh]
outside: can we sit outside? können wir
  draußen sitzen? [kurrnen veer drōwssen zitsen]
over: over here/there hier/dort drüben
  [heer/dort drōben]
  over 40 über vierzig [ōber feer-tsik]
  it's all over es ist aus [ess isst ōwss]
overboard: man overboard! Mann über Bord!
  [man ōber bort]
overcharge: you've overcharged me Sie haben
  mir zu viel berechnet [zee hah-ben meer tsoo
  feel buh-resh-net]
overcooked zu lange gekocht [tsoo lang-uh
  gheh-kokt]
overexposed überbelichtet [ōber-buh-likt-et]
overnight *(stay, travel)* über Nacht [ōber nahkt]

oversleep verschlafen [fair-shl*ah*-fen]
    I overslept ich habe verschlafen [ish hah-buh
    fair-shlah-fen]
overtake überholen [oober-hole-en]
owe: what do I owe you? was bin ich Ihnen
    schuldig? [vass bin ish ee-nen sh*oo*ldi*k*]
own *(adjective)* eigen [eye-ghen]
    my own car mein eigenes Auto
    I'm on my own ich bin allein hier [ish bin
    al-ine heer]
owner der Eigentümer [eye-ghen-t*oo*mer]
oxygen der Sauerstoff [z*ow*-er-shtoff]
oyster die Auster [*ow*-ster]
pack: I haven't packed yet ich habe noch nicht
    gepackt [ish h*ah*h-buh no*k* nisht gheh-packt]
package tour die Pauschalreise
    [p*ow*-sh*ah*l-ry-zuh]
page *(of book)* die Seite [zy-tuh]
    could you page him? können Sie ihn
    ausrufen lassen? [kurrnen zee een
    *ow*ss-roofen...]
pain der Schmerz [shmairts]
    I've got a pain in my... mir tut mein...
    weh [meer toot mine...vay]
    painkillers schmerzstillende Mittel
    [schmairts-shtill-end-uh...]
painting das Gemälde [gheh-m*eh*l-duh]
pair das Paar [par]
pajamas der Schlafanzug [schl*ah*f-an-tsoog]
pale blaß [blass]
pancake der Pfannkuchen [pfan-koo*k*en]
panties das Höschen [hurrs-shen]
pants die Hose [hoh-zuh]
    (underpants) die Unterhose [*oo*nter-hoh-zuh]
paper das Papier [pa-p*eer*]
    (newspaper) die Zeitung [tsyt*oo*ng]
parcel das Paket [pa-kayt]
pardon *(didn't understand)* wie bitte? [vee
    bittuh]
    I beg your pardon *(sorry)* Entschuldigung
    [ent-sh*oo*ld-ee-g*oo*ng]

parents: my parents meine Eltern
park der Park
  where can I park? wo kann ich parken?
  [voh . . .]
Parken nur mit Parkscheibe *parking permit*
  required
Parken verboten *no parking*
parking lot der Parkplatz
  (garage) das Parkhaus [park-hōwss]
Parkplatz *parking lot*
part ein Teil [ine tile]
partner der Partner
party *(group)* die Gruppe [grœp-uh]
  (travel) die Gesellschaft [gheh-zell-shafft]
  (celebration) die Party
  I'm with the . . . party ich bin mit
  der . . . Gruppe hier
pass *(mountain)* der Paß [pas]
passable *(road)* passierbar [pas-eer-bar]
passenger ein Reisender [ry-zender]
  (on ship, plane) ein Passagier [pass-ajeer]
passerby ein Passant
passport der Paß [pas]
past: in the past früher [frō-er]
pastry *(dough)* der Teig [tyg]
path der Weg [vayg]
patient: be patient Geduld! [gheh-dœlt]
pattern das Muster [mœster]
pavement der Gehsteig [gay-shtyg]
pay bezahlen [buh-tsahlen]
  may I pay, please? ich möchte gerne zahlen
  [ish murrshtuh gairn-uh tsahlen]
» *TRAVEL TIP: in bars, pubs, etc. it's usual to pay*
  when you're leaving and not when you order
pea eine Erbse [erp-suh]
peace der Frieden [free-den]
peach ein Pfirsich [pfeer-zish]
peanuts Erdnüsse [airt-nœss-uh]
pear eine Birne [beer-nuh]
pebble ein Kieselstein [kee-zel-shtine]
pedal das Pedal [pay-dahl]

pedestrian ein Fußgänger [fooss-genger]
   pedestrian crossing der Fußgängerüberweg
   [fooss-genger-ōōber-vayg]
» *TRAVEL TIP: be warned, the Germans take the*
   red lights for pedestrians rather more seriously
   than we do; on the spot fines can happen
peg der Stift [shtift]
   (mountaineering) der Haken [hah-ken]
pelvis das Becken
pen der Kugelschreiber [kooghel-shryber]
   have you got a pen? haben Sie etwas zum
   Schreiben? [hah-ben zee etvass tsōōm
   shryben]
pencil ein Bleistift [bly-shtift]
penicillin das Penizillin [pen-its-illeen]
penknife das Taschenmesser
penpal ein Brieffreund [breef-froynt]
people die Leute [loy-tuh]
   the German people die Deutschen
   [doyt-shen]
pepper der Pfeffer
   green/red pepper der grüne/rote Paprika
   [grōōnuh/roh-tuh . . .]
peppermint das Pfefferminz
per: per night/week/person pro Nacht/Woche/
   Person [proh nahkt/vok-uh/pair-zohn]
percent Prozent [proh-tsent]
perfect perfekt [pair-fekt]
   the perfect vacation der ideale Urlaub
   [dair ee-day-ahl-uh oorlōwp]
perfume das Parfüm [parfōōm]
perhaps vielleicht [fee-lysht]
period der Zeitraum [tsyt-rōwm]
   (medical) die Periode [pay-ree-oh-duh]
perm die Dauerwelle [dōw-er-vell-uh]
permanent dauernd [dōw-ernt]
permit *(noun)* die Genehmigung
   [gheh-nay-migōōng]
person die Person [pair-zohn]
   in person persönlich [pair-zurrn-lish]

pharmacy die Apotheke [–taykuh]
» *TRAVEL TIP: pharmacies display a notice about
    night service (Nachtdiehst) and Sunday service
    (Sonntagsdienst)*
phone *see* **telephone**
photograph die Fotografie [foto-gra-*fee*]
  **would you take a photograph of
  us?** würden Sie ein Bild von uns machen?
  [vōōrden zee ine bilt fon ∞nz mah-*k*en]
piano das Klavier [kla-*veer*]
pickpocket der Taschendieb [tashen-deep]
picture ein Bild [bilt]
pie die Pastete [pas-*tay*-tuh]
  (sweet) der Obstkuchen [ohpst-koo*k*en]
  apple pie der Apfelkuchen [apfel-koo*k*en]
piece das Stück [sht∞ck]; **a piece of cheese** ein
  Stück Käse [ine sht∞ck kay-zuh]
  a big piece ein großes Stück
pig das Schwein [shvine]
pigeon die Taube [tōw-buh]
pile-up die Massenkarambolage
  [massen-karambo-l*a*h-juh]
pill eine Tablette [tab-lettuh]
  do you take the pill? nimmst du die Pille?
  [. . . pill-uh]
pillow das Kissen
pin die (Steck)nadel [(shteck)n*a*h-del]
pineapple eine Ananas
pink *(adjective)* rosa
pint die Pint
» *TRAVEL TIP: 1 pint = 0.47 liters*
pipe die Pfeife [pfy-fuh]
  pipe tobacco der Pfeifentabak [pfy-fen-tabak]
  (sink, etc.) das Rohr [ror]
piston der Kolben
pity: it's a pity das ist schade [dass isst
  shah-duh]
Pkw [pay-ka-vay] = *Personenkraftwagen*
  (private) motor car
place der Platz *(town)* der Ort

is this place taken? ist hier besetzt? [isst heer buh-zetst]

do you know any good place to go? wissen Sie, wo man hingehen könnte? [vissen zee voh man hin-gay-en kurrnt-uh]

plain *(food)* (gut)bürgerlich [(goot)bōōr-gher-lish]
(not patterned) einfarbig [ine-farbik]

plane das Flugzeug [floog-tsoyg]

plant die Pflanze [pflannts-uh]
(factory) das Werk [vairk]
(equipment) die Anlagen [an-lah-ghen]

plaster *(med)* der Gips [ghips] *see* **sticking**

plastic Plastik
plastic wrap das Cellophan [tsello-fahn]

plate der Teller

platform der Bahnsteig [bahn-shtyg]
which platform please? welches Gleis, bitte? [velshes glice bittuh]

play *(verb)* spielen [shpeelen]

pleasant angenehm

please: could you please...? könnten Sie, bitte,...? [kurrnten zee bittuh]
(yes) please ja, bitte [yah bittuh]

pleasure das Vergnügen [fair-guh-nōō-ghen]
my pleasure gern geschehen [gairn gheh-shay-en]

plenty: plenty of... viel... [feel]
thank you, that's plenty danke, das reicht [dan-kuh dass rysht]

pliers eine Zange [tsang-uh]

plug *(electrical)* ...der Stecker [shtecker]
(car) die Zündkerze [tsōōnt-kairts-uh]
(bathroom) der Stöpsel [shturrp-sel]

plum eine Pflaume [pflōwm-uh]

plus plus [plooss]

p.m. nachmittags [nahk-mittahgs]

pneumonia die Lungenentzündung [loong-en-ent-tsōōndoong]

poached egg ein pochiertes Ei [posheertes eye]

pocket die Tasche [tash-uh]

point: could you point to it? könnten Sie
darauf deuten? [kurrnen zee darōwf doyten]
four point six vier komma sechs
[feer . . . zex]
points *(car)* die Unterbrecherkontakte
[ōonter-bresher-kontakt-uh]
police die Polizei [polits-*e*ye]
get the police holen Sie die Polizei [hoh-len
zee dee . . .]
policeman der Polizist [polits-ist]
police station die (Polizei)wache [. . . vah*k*-uh]
» *TRAVEL TIP: dial 211*
polish *(noun: shoes)* die Schuhcreme
[sh*oo*-kray-muh]
could you polish my shoes? könnten Sie
meine Schuhe putzen lassen? [kurrnten zee
mine-uh shoo-uh p*oo*tsen lassen]
polite höflich [hurrf-lish]
politics die Politik [poli-t*ee*k]
polluted verschmutzt [fair-shm*ōo*tst]
pool *(swimming)* das Schwimmbad
[shv*i*mm-baht]
poor: I'm very poor ich bin sehr arm [ish bin
zair . . .]; **poor quality** schlechte Qualität
[shle*k*t-uh kval-ee-t*a*yt]
popular beliebt [buh-l*ee*pt]
population die Bevölkerung
[buh-f*u*rlk-kuh-r*oo*ng]
pork das Schweinefleisch [shvine-uh-flysh]
port *(harbor)* der Hafen [h*a*h-fen]
(not starboard) Backbord [–bort]
(drink) der Portwein
porter der Portier [por-tee-ay]
(rail, airport) der Gepäckträger
[gheh-p*e*ck-tray-gher]
portrait das Porträt [por-tr*a*y]
posh vornehm [f*o*r-naym]
possible möglich [murr-glish]
could you possibly . . . ? könnten Sie
eventuell . . . ? [kurrn-ten zee ay-vent-oo-*e*
postcard die Postkarte [posst-kar-tuh]

....

post office das Postamt
» *TRAVEL TIP: post offices generally open from
8:00–6:00 Monday to Friday and 8:00 to 12:00
on Saturdays*
potato die Kartoffel
  potato chips die Chips
pottery die Töpferei [turrpfer-eye]
  (pots) die Töpferwaren [turrpfer-vah-ren]
  (glazed) die Keramik [kay-rah-mik]
pound das Pfund [pfoont]
» *TRAVEL TIP: conversion:* $\dfrac{pounds}{11} \times 5 = kilos$

pounds	1	3	5	6	7	8	9
kilos	0.45	1.4	2.3	2.7	3.2	3.6	4.1

NB: *a German Pfund = 500 grams*
pour: it's pouring es grießt [ess geesst]
powder das Pulver [pool-ver]
  (face) das Puder [poo-der]
power outage der Stromausfall
  [shtrohm-ōwss-fal]
prefer: I prefer this one das gefällt mir besser
  [... gheh-fellt meer ...]
  I'd prefer to ... ich würde lieber ...
  [ish vōōr-duh lee-ber]
  I'd prefer a ... ich hätte lieber ein ...
  [ish het-uh lee-ber ine ...]
pregnant schwanger [shvanger]
prescription das Rezept [rets-ept]
present: at present zur Zeit [tsoor tsite]
  present company excepted Anwesende
  ausgeschlossen [anvay-zend-uh
  ōwss-gheh-shlossen]
  here's a present for you ein Geschenk für
  Sie [ine gheh-shenk fōōr zee]
president der Präsident [pray-zident]
press: could you press these? könnten Sie sie
  bügeln? [kurrnten zee zee bōō-gheln]
pretty hübsch [hōōpsh]
  it's pretty good es ist ganz gut [... gants
  goot]
price der Preis [price]

priest der Priester [preester]
print *(photo)* ein Abzug [app-tsoog]
printed matter Drucksache [drock-zah*k*-uh]
prison das Gefängnis [gheh-*f*engnis]
private privat [pree-v*a*ht]
probably wahrscheinlich [vahr-sh*i*ne-lish]
problem das Problem [prob-l*a*ym]
product das Produkt [prod*oo*ckt]
profit der Gewinn [gheh-v*i*nn]
promise: do you promise? versprechen Sie es?
   [fair-shpreshen zee ess]
   I promise ehrlich! [*ai*r-lish]
pronounce: how do you pronounce it? wie
   spricht man das aus? [vee shprisht man dass
   *ō*wss]
propeller der Propeller
properly richtig [r*i*k-t*i*k]
property das Eigentum [*eye*-ghen-toom]
   (land) der Besitz [buh-z*i*ts]
prostitute die Prostituierte [prostit-oo-*ee*r-tuh]
protect schützen [sh*ō*tsen]
Protestant evangelisch [ay-van-g*a*y-lish]
proud stolz [shtolts]
prove: I can prove it ich kann es beweisen
   [ish kann ess buh-v*i*se-en]
public: the public die Öffentlichkeit
   [urrfent-lish-kite]
   public holiday gesetzlicher Feiertag
   [gheh-zets-lisher fire-tahg]
» *TRAVEL TIP: public holidays are:*
   New Year's Day *Neujahr*
   Good Friday *Karfreitag*
   Easter Monday *Ostermontag*
   May Day *Erster Mai*
   Ascension Day *Christi Himmelfahrt*
   Whit Monday *Pfingstmontag*
   National Unity Day *Tag der deutschen Einheit*
   (17th June)
   Day of Prayer and Repentance *Buß-und Bettag*
   (mid Nov)

Christmas Day 1. *(erster) Weihnachtsfeiertag*
Boxing Day 2. *(zweiter) Weihnachtsfeiertag; in
the mainly Catholic parts there is also:*
Epiphany *Dreikönige*
Corpus Christi *Fronleichnam*
Assumption *Mariä Himmelfahrt*
pudding der Pudding
  (dessert) der Nachtisch [nah*k*tish]
pull *(verb)* ziehen [tsee-en]; **he pulled out in
  front of me** er ist vor mir ausgeschert [air
  isst for meer ṓwss-gheh-shayrt]
pump die Pumpe [pōm-puh]
punctual pünktlich [pṓnkt-lish]
puncture die Reifenpanne [rye-fen-pan-uh]
pure rein [rine]
purple lila [lee-lah]
purse das Portemonnaie [port-mon-*a*y]
push *(verb)* schieben [sheeben]
put: where can I put . . . ? wo kann ich . . .
  hintun? [voh kann ish . . . *h*intoon]
  where have you put it? wo haben Sie es
  hingetan? [voh h*a*h-ben zee es *h*in-gheh-tahn]
quality die Qualität [kval-ee-t*a*yt]
quarantine die Quarantäne [kvar-an-t*a*yn-uh]
quarter ein Viertel [f*ee*r-tel]
  a quarter of an hour eine Viertelstunde
  [ine-uh feer-tel shtōn-duh]
quay der Kai [kye]
question die Frage [frah-guh]
quick schnell [shnel]
  that was quick das ging schnell
quiet ruhig [roo-i*k*]; *(not noisy)* still [shtill]
quite ganz [gants]
  quite a lot ziemlich viel [tseem-lish feel]
race das Rennen
radiator der Kühler [kōōler]
  (heater) der Heizkörper [*h*ites-kurr-per]
radio das Radio [r*a*h-dee-oh]
Radweg cycle path
rain der Regen [r*a*y-ghen]
  it's raining es regnet [ess rayg-net]

raincoat der Regenmantel
rain boots die Gummistiefel [goomee-shteefel]
rally *(car)* die Rallye
rape die Vergewaltigung [fair-gheh-val-tigoong]
rare selten [z−]; *(steak)* blutig [bloo-tik]
raspberries Himbeeren [him-bair-en]
rat die Ratte [rat-uh]
rather: I'd rather sit here ich würde lieber hier
sitzen [ish voor-duh lee-ber heer zitsen]
I'd rather have a ... ich hätte lieber ein ...
[ish het-uh lee-ber ine]
I'd rather not lieber nicht! [lee-ber nisht]
it's rather hot es ist ganz schön heiß [ess isst
gants shurrn hice]
Rauchen verboten *no smoking*
Raucher *smoking compartment*
raw roh
razor der Rasierapparat [ra-zeer−]
razor blades Rasierklingen
read: you read it lesen Sie es [lay-zen zee ess]
something to read etwas zu lesen [et-vass
tsoo ...]
ready: when will it be ready? wann ist es
fertig [van isst ess fair-tik]
I'm not ready yet ich bin noch nicht fertig
[ish bin nok nisht ...]
real *(genuine)* echt [esht]
really wirklich [veerk-lish]
rearview mirror der Rückspiegel
[rook-shpee-ghel]
reasonable vernünftig [fair-noonf-tik]
receipt die Quittung [kvit-oong]
can I have a receipt, please? kann ich, bitte,
eine Quittung haben? [kan ish bittuh
ine-uh ... hah-ben]
recently kürzlich [koorts-lish]
reception *(hotel)* der Empfang
at reception am Empfang
receptionist der Empfangschef
(lady) die Empfangsdame [−dah-muh]
rechts fahren *keep right*

recipe das Rezept [rets-ept]
recommend: can you recommend...? können
Sie ... empfehlen? [kurrn-en zee ...
emp-*fay*-len]
record *(music)* die Platte [plat-uh]
red rot [roht]
reduction *(in price)* die Ermäßigung
[air-m*a*ce-ee-g*oo*ng]
refrigerator der Kühlschank [k*oo*l–]
refuse: I refuse ich weigere mich [ish
vy-guh-ruh mish]
region das Gebiet [gheh-b*eet*]
  in this region in diesem Gebiet [in
  dee-zem ...]
registered: I want to send it registered ich
möchte das per Einschreiben schicken [ish
murrsh-tuh das pair ine-shryben shicken]
regret das Bedauern [buh-d*ó*wern]
  I have no regrets ich bereue nichts [ish
  buh-r*oy*-uh nix]
relax: I just want to relax ich möchte mich nur
entspannen [ish murrsh-tuh mish noor
ent-shpannen]
  relax! ganz ruhig! [gants roo-i*k*]
remember: don't you remember? wissen Sie
das nicht mehr? [vissen zee das nisht mair]
  I'll always remember ich werde es nie
  vergessen [ish vair-duh ess nee fair-g*h*essen]
  something to remember you by ein
  Andenken an dich [ine ... dish]
rent: can I rent a car/boat/bicycle? kann ich
ein Auto/Boot/Fahrrad mieten? [... meeten]
repair: can you repair it? können Sie es
reparieren? [kurrn-en zee ess rep-a-*ree*-ren]
repeat: could you repeat that? könnten Sie
das wiederholen [kurrn-ten zee dass
veeder-h*o*le-en]
reputation der Ruf [roof]
rescue *(verb)* retten
reservation die Reservierung [rez-air-v*ee*-r*oo*ng]

I want to make a reservation for...
(hotel) ich möchte ein Zimmer für... bestellen
[ish murrsh-tuh ine tsimmer fōōr...
buh-shtellen]
(theater) ich möchte einen Platz reservieren
für... [... ine-en plats rez-air-vee-ren...]
reserve: can I reserve a seat/table? kann ich
einen Platz/Tisch reservieren? [kan ish ine-en
plats/tish rez-air-vee-ren]
  can I reserve a seat for...? kann ich einen
  Platz für... bestellen? [... fōōr... buhshtellen]
  I'd like to reserve a table for two ich
  möchte gerne einen Tisch für zwei bestellen
  [ish murrshtuh gairn-uh ine-en tish fōōr tsvy
  buh-shtellen]
responsible verantwortlich [fair-ant-vort-lish]
rest: I've come here for a rest ich bin hier,
um mal auszuspannen [ish bin heer oom mal
ōwss-tsoo-shpannen]
  you keep the rest der Rest ist für Sie
  [... isst fōōr zee]
rest room die Toilette [twa-lettuh]
  where is the rest room? wo ist die Toilette?
  [voh ist dee...]
  public rest room öffentliche Toilette [urrfent-
  lish-uh twa-lettuh]
  » *TRAVEL TIP: see* **toilet**
restaurant ein Restaurant [−rong]
retail price der Einzelhandelspreis
[ine-tsel-handels-price]
retired pensioniert [pen-zee-oh-neert]
reverse charge call ein R-Gespräch
[air-ghehshpraysh]
reverse gear der Rückwärtsgang [rōōck-vairts−]
rheumatism der Rheumatismus
[roy-ma-tismooss]
rib eine Rippe [rip-uh]
rice der Reis [rice]
rich reich [rysh] *(food)* schwer [shvair]
ridiculous lächerlich [lesh-er-lish]

right: that's right das stimmt [dass shtimmt]
  you're right Sie haben recht [zee hah-ben resht]
  on the right rechts [reshts]
  right here genau hier [gheh-nōw heer]
  right now sofort [zoh-fort]
  right-hand drive rechts gesteuert [reshts ghen-shtoy-ert]
ring *(on finger)* der Ring
ripe reif [rife]
rip-off: it's a rip-off das ist Wucher! [dass isst vook-er]
river der Fluß [flōoss]
road die Straße [shtrass-uh]
  which is the road to . . . ? wo geht es nach . . . ? [voh gayt ess nahk . . .]
  roadhog der Verkehrsrowdy [fair-kairs−]
rob: I've been robbed ich bin bestohlen worden [ish bin buh-shtole-en vorden]
rock der Fels [felz]
  whisky on the rocks Whisky mit Eis [. . . ice]
roll *(bread)* ein Brötchen [brurrt-shen]
Roman Catholic (römisch-) katholisch [(rurr-mish) kat-olish]
romantic romantisch [−tish]
roof das Dach [dahk]
room das Zimmer [tsimmer]
  have you got a (single/double) room? haben Sie ein (Einzel/Doppel)zimmer? [hah-ben zee ine (ine-tsel/doppel) . . .]
  for one night/for three nights für eine Nacht/für drei Nächte [fōor ine-uh nahkt/fōor dry neshte]
  YOU MAY THEN HEAR . . .
  mit Bad oder ohne? *with or without bath?*
  tut mir leid, wir sind voll ausgebucht/wir haben nichts mehr frei *sorry, we're full*
room service der Zimmerservice [tsimmer-serviss]
rope das Seil [zile]
rose die Rose [roh-zuh]

rough rauh [rōw]
roughly ungefähr [ŏon-gheh-fair]
roulette das Roulett(e)
round *(circular)* rund [rŏont]
roundabout der Kreisverkehr [krɪce-fair-kair]
round-trip: a round-trip ticket to . . . eine
  Rückfahrkarte nach . . . [rŏock-fahr-kartuh
  nahk]
route die Strecke [shtreck-uh]
  which is the prettiest/fastest route? was ist
  die schönste/schnellste Strecke?
  [. . . shurrn-stuh/shnel-stuh . . .]
rowboat das Ruderboot [rooder-boht]
rubber der Gummi [gŏo-mee]
  rubberband ein Gummiband [−bannt]
rudder das Ruder [rooder]
rude unhöflich [ŏon-hurrf-lish]
Ruhetag closed all day
ruin die Ruine [roo-een-uh]
rum ein Rum [rŏom]
  rum and coke Cola mit Rum
run: hurry, run! beeil dich, lauf! [buh-ile dish
  lōwf]
  I've run out of gas/money mir ist das
  Benzin/Geld ausgegangen [meer isst dass
  ben-tseen/gelt ōws-gheh-gang-en]
Sackgasse cul-de-sac
sad traurig [trōw-rɪk]
safe sicher [zisher]
  will it be safe here? ist es hier sicher? [isst es
  heer . . .]
  is it safe to swim here? kann man hier ohne
  Gefahr schwimmen? [. . . oh-nuh gheh-fahr
  shvimmen]
safety die Sicherheit [zisher-hite]
  safety pin eine Sicherheitsnadel [−snah-del]
sail segeln [zay-gheln]
  can we go sailing? können wir segeln gehen?
  [kurrn-en veer . . . gay-en]
sailor ein Seemann [zay-man]
  (sports) ein Segler [zaygler]

....

salad ein Salat [zal-aht]
salami die Salami [z–]
sale: is it for sale? kann man das kaufen?
[. . . kŏw-fen]
  salesclerk *(male)* der Verkäufer [fair-k*oy*-fer]
  (female) die Verkäuferin
salmon der Lachs [lax]
salt das Salz [zalts]
same der-/die-/dasselbe [dair-/dee-/dass-zelbuh]
  the same again, please das gleiche noch
  mal, bitte [dass glysh-uh no*k* mal bittuh]
  the same to you (danke) gleichfalls [(dankuh)
  glysh-falz]
sand der Sand [zannt]
sandal die Sandale [zan-d*a*hl-uh]
sandwich ein Sandwich
sanitary napkin die Damenbinde
  [dah-men-bin-duh]
satisfactory befriedigend [buh-freed-ee-ghent]
Saturday Samstag [zamz-tahg]
sauce die Soße [zoh-suh]
  saucepan der Kochtopf [ko*k*-topf]
saucer der Unterteller [œnter–]
sauna die Sauna [zŏw-na]
sausage die Wurst [v*oo*rst]
save *(life)* retten
say: how do you say . . . in German? was
  heißt . . . auf Deutsch? [vass hysst . . . ŏwf
  doytsh]
  what did he say? was hat er gesagt? [vass
  hat air gheh-zahgt]
scarf der Schal [shahl]
  (neck scarf) das Halstuch [halz-too*k*]
  (head scarf) das Kopftuch
scenery die Landschaft [lannt-shafft]
schedule der Zeitplan [tsite-plahn]
  on/behind schedule pünktlich/verspätet
  [pŏonkt-lish/fair-shp*a*ytet]
  (work) **on schedule** programmgemäß
  [progr*a*m-gheh-mace]; **behind schedule** im
  Verzug [fair-ts*oo*g]

scheduled flight der Linienflug
[leen-ee-en-floog]
Schlafwagen sleeper
Schließfächer luggage lockers
Schlußverkauf sale
schnapps ein Schnaps
» TRAVEL TIP: *can be made from practically*
anything; try North German "Korn" (grain),
Black Forest "Kirsch" (cherries), or
"Steinhäger" [shtine-hay-gher] *(juniper berries)*
school die Schule [shool-uh]
scissors: a pair of scissors eine Schere [ine-uh
shay-ruh]
scooter der (Motor)roller
Scot Schotte [shot-uh] *(woman)* Schottin
Scotland Schottland [shott-lannt]
Scottish schottisch [shottish]
scrambled eggs Rührei [rōōr-eye]
scratch der Kratzer
scream *(verb)* schreien [shry-en]
screw die Schraube [shrōw-buh]
  screwdriver ein Schraubenzieher
  [–ben-tsee-er]
sea das Meer [mayr]; **by the sea** am Meer
seafood Meeresfrüchte [mayr-es-frōōkt-uh]
search die Suche [zook-uh]
  search party die Suchmannschaft
  [zook-man-shafft]
seasick: I get seasick ich werde seekrank [ish
vairduh zay–]
seaside: let's go to the seaside fahren wir ans
Meer! [fahren veer anz mayr]
season die Saison [sez-ong]
  in the high/low season in der Hochsaison/
  Nebensaison [in dair hohk–/nay-ben–]
seasoning das Gewürz [gheh-vōōrts]
seat der (Sitz)platz
  is this somebody's seat? sitzt hier jemand?
  [zitst heer yay-mannt]
  seat belt der Sicherheitsgurt
  [zisher-hites-gœrt]

seaweed der Tang
second *(adjective)* zweite [tsvy-tuh]
  (time) die Sekunde [zeck-oonduh]
  just a second Moment!
  second class zweite Klasse [. . . klass-uh . . .]
  second hand gebraucht [gheh-brŏwkt]
see sehen [zay-en]
  oh, I see ach so! [ahk zoh]
  have you seen . . . ? haben Sie . . . gesehen?
  [hah-ben zee . . . gheh-zay-en]
  can I see the room? kann ich mir das
  Zimmer anschauen? [kan ish meer dass
  tsimmer an-shŏw-en]
seem scheinen [shine-en]
  it seems so so sieht es aus [zoh zeet ess ŏwss]
seldom selten [zelten]
self: self-service Selbstbedienung
  [zelpst-buh-deen-oong]
sell verkaufen [fair-kŏwfen]
send schicken [shicken]
senior citizen der Rentner
sensitive empfindlich [emp-finnt-lish]
sentimental sentimental
separate getrennt [gheh–]
  I'm separated wir leben getrennt [veer
  lay-ben . . .]
  can we pay separately? können wir getrennt
  zahlen? [kurrn-en veer . . . tsah-len]
September September [z–]
serious ernst [airnst]
  I'm serious ich meine das ernst [ish my-nuh
  dass . . .]
  this is serious das ist ernst
  is it serious, doctor? ist es schlimm? [isst ess
  shlim]
service: the service was excellent/poor der
  Service war ausgezeichnet/schlecht [dair
  serviss vahr ŏwss-gheh-tsysh-net/shlessht]
  service station die Tankstelle (mit
  Reparaturwerkstatt) [tank-shtelluh (mit
  rep-a-rah-toor-vairk-shtat)]

several mehrere [mair-uh-ruh]

sexy sexy

shade: in the shade im Schatten [. . . shat-en]

shake schütteln [shoot-eln]

   to shake hands die Hand schütteln [dee hannt . . .]

» *TRAVEL TIP: it is normal to shake hands each time you meet someone and when you leave someone*

shallow seicht [zysht]

shame: what a shame wie schade! [vee shah-duh]

shampoo ein Shampoo(n); **shampoo and set** Waschen und Legen [vashen oont lay-ghen]

share *(room)* teilen [tile-en]

   (table) gemeinsam nehmen [gheh-mine-zahm nay-men]

sharp scharf [sharf]

shave rasieren [ra-zee-ren]

   shaver der Rasierapparat [ra-zeer–]

   shaving cream der Rasierschaum [–showm]

she sie [zee] **she is** sie ist [zee isst]

sheep das Schaf [shahf]

sheet das Leintuch [line-took]

   you haven't changed my sheets Sie haben die Bettwäsche nicht gewechselt [zee hah-ben-dee bett-vesh-un nisht gheh-vek-selt]

shelf das Regal [ray-gahl]

shell die Schale [shah-luh]

   (on beach) die Muschel mooshel]

   shellfish Meeresfrüchte [mayr-es-froosh-tuh]

shelter *(noun)* der Unterstand [oonter-shtannt]

sherry ein Sherry

ship das Schiff [shif]

shirt das Hemd [hemmt]

shock *(noun: surprise)* der Schock

   what a shock so ein Schreck! [zoh ine shreck]

   I got an electric shock from the . . . ich habe von dem . . . einen Schlag bekommen [ish hah-buh fon daym . . . ine-nen shlahg buh–]

shock absorber der Stoßdämpfer
[sht*o*hss-dem-pfer]
shoe der Schuh [shoo]
» *TRAVEL TIP: shoe sizes:*

US	6/6½	7/7½	8	8½	9/9½	10
Germany	38	39	40	41	42	43

shop das Geschäft [gheh-sh*e*fft]
   I've some shopping to do ich muß noch ein
   paar Einkäufe erledigen [ish m*oo*ss no*k*
   *i*ne-koy-fuh air-l*a*y-dig-en]
» *TRAVEL TIP: shops generally open from*
   9:00–6:30; closed Saturday afternoon except the
   first Saturday in the month
shore das Ufer [oofer]
   (sea) der Strand [shtrannt]
short kurz [k*oo*rts]
   I'm three short mir fehlen drei [meer f*a*y-len
   dry]
   shortcut eine Abkürzung [*i*ne-uh
   *a*pp-k$\overline{oo}$rts-*oo*ng]
shorts die Shorts
shoulder die Schulter [sh*oo*lter]
shout rufen [roofen]
show: please show me bitte zeigen Sie es mir
   [bittuh tsy-ghen zee ess meer]
shower: with shower mit Dusche [mit d*oo*sh-uh]
shrimp eine Garnele [gar-n*a*y-luh]
shrink: it's shrunk es ist eingegangen [ess isst
   *i*ne-gheh-gang-en]
shut *(verb)* schließen [shlee-sen]
   shut up! halt den Mund! [hallt dayn m*oo*nt]
shy schüchtern [sh$\overline{oo}$sh-tern]
sick krank
   I feel sick mir ist schlecht [meer isst shlesht]
   he's been sick er hat gebrochen [air hat
   gheh-bro*k*-en]
side die Seite [zy-tuh]
   side street die Nebenstraße
   [n*a*y-ben-shtrahss-uh]
   by the side of the road an der Straße
sight: out of sight außer Sicht [$\overline{o}$wsser zisht]

the sights of... die Sehenswürdigkeiten von... [zay-enz-vōord-i*k*-kite-en fon]
sight-seeing tour eine Rundreise [rōont-ry-zuh] *(of town)* eine Stadtrundfahrt [shtat-rōont-fahrt]
sign *(notice)* das Schild [shilt]
signal: he didn't signal er hat kein Zeichen gegeben [air hat kine tsyshen gheh-gay-ben]
signature die Unterschrift [ōonter-shrift]
silk die Seide [zy-duh]
silly dumm [dōomm]
silver das Silber [zilber]
similar ähnlich [*a*yn-lish]
simple einfach [ine-fah*k*]
since: since last week seit letzter Woche [zite lets-ter voc*k*-uh]; *(because)* weil [vile]
sincere aufrichtig [ōwf-ri*k*-ti*k*]
   yours sincerely mit freundlichen Grüßen
sing singen [zing-en]
single: single room ein Einzelzimmer [ine-tsel-tsimmer]
   I'm single ich bin ledig [ish bin l*a*y-di*k*]
sink: it sank es ist gesunken [ess isst gheh-zōonken]
sir Herr
sister: my sister meine Schwester [mine-uh shvester]
sit: can I sit here? kann ich mich hierher setzen? [kan ish mish heer-hair zetsen]
size die Größe [grurr-suh]
ski *(noun)* der Ski [shee]; *(verb)* skifahren
   skiing das Skifahren
   ski boots die Skistiefel [–shteefel]
   ski lift der Skilift
   ski pants die Skihose [–hoh-zuh]
   ski pole der Skistock [–shtock]
   ski slope/run der Skihang/die Skipiste
   ski wax das Skiwachs [–vax]
skid schleudern [shl*o*y-dern]
skin die Haut [hōwt]
skirt der Rock

sky der Himmel
sledge der Schlitten [sh−]
sleep: I can't sleep ich kann nicht schlafen [ish
    kan nisht shl*a*h-fen]
    sleeper *(rail)* der Schlafwagen
    [shl*a*f-vah-ghen]
    sleeping bag der Schlafsack
    sleeping pill die Schlaftablette [−lettuh]
    YOU MAY HEAR...
    haben Sie gut geschlafen? *did you sleep*
    well?
sleeve der Armel [*a*ir-mel]
slide *(photo)* das Dia [d*ee*-ah]
slippery glatt
slow langsam [l*a*ng-zahm]
    could you speak a little slower? könnten
    Sie etwas langsamer sprechen? [kurrn-ten zee
    et-vass l*a*ng-zahmer shpreshen]
small klein [kline]
    small change das Kleingeld [−gelt]
smell: there's a funny smell hier riecht es
    komisch [heer ree*k*t ess koh-mish]
    it smells es stinkt [ess shtinkt]
smile *(verb)* lächeln [lesh-eln]
smoke *(noun)* der Rauch [r*ō*w*k*]
    do you smoke? rauchen Sie? [r*ō*w*k*en
    zee]
    can I smoke? darf ich rauchen?
smooth glatt
snack: can we just have a snack? können wir
    einen Imbiß bekommen? [kurrn-en veer ine-en
    im-biss buh-kommen]
» *TRAVEL TIP: you will find plenty of indoor and*
    outdoor snackbars called "Schnellimbiß" or
    "Imbißstube," which sell sausages, french fries,
    etc.
snow *(noun)* der Schnee [shnay]
    it's snowing es schneit [ess shnite]
» *TRAVEL TIP: snow chains (Schneeketten) can be*
    hired from ADAC depots

stopover die Zwischenstation
[tsvishen-shtats-ee-ohn]
  do you stop near...? halten Sie in der Nähe
  von...? [hal-ten zee in dair nay-uh fon]
storm der Sturm [shtoorm]
...ist strafbar ...is an offense
stove der Herd [hairt]
straight gerade [gheh-rah-duh]
  go straight on gehen Sie geradeaus
  [gay-en zee gheh-rah-duh-öwss]
  straight whisky Whisky pur [...poor]
strange fremd [fremmt]
  (odd) seltsam [zelt-zahm]
stranger der Fremde [frem-duh]
  I'm a stranger here ich bin fremd hier [ish
  bin fremmt heer]
strawberries Erdbeeren [airt-bair-en]
street die Straße [shtrahss-uh]
string: have you got any string? haben Sie
  Schnur? [hah-ben zee shnoor]
stroke: he's had a stroke er hat einen
  Schlag(anfall) bekommen [air hat ine-en
  shlahg-an-fal buh-kommen]
strong stark [shtark]
student der Student [shtoo-dent]; *(girl)* die
  Studentin
stung: I've been stung ich bin gestochen
  worden [ish bin gheh-shtoken vorden]
stupid dumm [doomm]
subway die Untergrundbahn, U-Bahn [oonter-
  groont-bahn, oo-bahn]
such: such a lot so viel [zoh feel]
suddenly plötzlich [plurrts-lish]
sugar der Zucker [tsoocker]
suit *(man's)* der Anzug [an-tsoog]
  (woman's) das Kostüm [kostöōm]
suitable passend [pas-ent]
suitcase der Koffer
summer der Sommer [zommer]
sun die Sonne [zonnuh]

in the sun in der Sonne
out of the sun im Schatten [shat-en]
sunbathe sonnenbaden [zonnen-bah-den]
sunburn der Sonnenbrand [−brannt]
sunglasses die Sonnenbrille [−brill-uh]
suntan lotion das Sonnenöl [−urrl]
Sunday Sonntag [zonn-tahg]
supermarket der Supermarkt [zooper−]
supper das Abendessen [ah-bent−]
sure: I'm not sure ich bin nicht sicher [ish bin
nisht zisher] **sure!** sicher!
are you sure? sind Sie sicher? [zinnt zee . . .]
surname der Zuname [tsoo-nah-muh]
swearword der Fluch [flook]
sweat (verb) schwitzen [shvitzen]
sweater der Pullover
sweet süß [zœss]
(dessert) der Nachtisch [nahk-tish]
swerve: I had to swerve ich mußte
ausschwenken [ish mœss-tuh ŏwss-shvenken]
swim: I'm going for a swim ich gehe
schwimmen [ish gay-uh shvimmen]
swimsuit der Badeanzug [bah-duh-an-tsoog]
swimming pool das Schwimmbad
[shvimm-baht]
Swiss Schweizer [shvy-tser]
(person) Schweizer; (woman) Schweizerin
switch (noun) der Schalter [shall-ter]
to switch on/off anschalten/abschalten
[an-shall-ten/app−]
Switzerland die Schweiz [shvites]
in Switzerland in der Schweiz
table ein Tisch [tish]
a table for 4 ein Tisch für vier [. . . fœr . . .]
table wine Tafelwein [tah-fel-vine]
take nehmen [nay-men]
can I take this with me? kann ich das
mitnehmen?
will you take me to the airport? bringen Sie
mich zum Flughafen? [. . . zee mish tsoom
floog-hah-fen]

how long will it take? wie lange dauert es?
[vee lang-uh dōwert ess]
somebody has taken my bags jemand hat
mein Gepäck mitgenommen [yay-mannt hat
mine gheh-peck mit-gheh-nommen]
can I take you out tonight? kann ich Sie für
heute abend einladen? [kan ish zee fōr hoy-tuh
ah-bent ine-lah-den]
talcum powder der (Körper)puder
[(kurr-per)pooder]
talk *(verb)* sprechen [shpreshen]
tall groß [grohss]
tampons die Tampons
tan die Bräune [broy-nuh]
tank *(of car)* der Tank
tape das Tonband [tohn-bannt]
tape recorder das Tonbandgerät [–gheh-
rayt]
tariff der Tarif [tah-reef]
(in hotels) die Preisliste [price-list-uh]
taste *(noun)* der Geschmack [gheh-shmack]
can I taste it? kann ist es versuchen? [kan ish
ess fair-zooken]
it tastes horrible/very nice das schmeckt
fürchterlich/sehr gut [dass shmeckt
fōrsh-terlish/zair goot]
taxi ein Taxi
will you get me a taxi? rufen Sie mir, bitte,
ein Taxi! [roofen zee meer bittuh . . .]
where can I get a taxi? wo bekomme ich ein
Taxi? [voh buh-kommuh ish . . .]
taxi driver der Taxifahrer
tea der Tee [tay]
could I have a cup/pot of tea? könnte ich
eine Tasse/ein Kännchen Tee haben?
[kurrn-tuh ish ine-uh tass-uh/ine ken-shen tay
hah-ben]
YOU MAY THEN HEAR . . .
mit Zitrone? *with lemon?*
no, with milk, please nein, mit Milch, bitte
[nine mit milsh bittuh]

teach: could you teach me? könnten Sie mir das beibringen? [kurrn-ten zee meer dass by-bringen]

could you teach me German? könnten Sie mir Deutsch beibringen? [. . . doytsh . . .]

teacher der Lehrer [lair-uh]
(woman) die Lehrerin

telegram ein Telegramm

I want to send a telegram ich möchte ein Telegramm schicken [ish murrsh-tuh . . .]

telephone *(noun)* das Telefon

telephone booth die Telefonzelle [–tselluh]

can I make a phone call? kann ich hier telefonieren? [. . . heer tele-foneer-en]

can I speak to . . . ? kann ich . . . sprechen? [. . . spreshen]

could you get the number for me? könnten Sie die Nummer für mich wählen? [kurrnten zee dee noomer foor mish vay-len]

telephone directory das Telefonbuch [–book]

» *TRAVEL TIP: lift receiver, insert money, dial; unused coins returned; for international calls look for boxes with green disc with "Ausland" or "International"; code for US is 001*

YOU MAY HEAR . . .

kein Anschluß unter dieser Nummer *number not in use*

bitte warten *please wait*

television das Fernsehen [fairn-zay-en]

I'd like to watch television ich möchte gerne fernsehen [ish murrsh-tuh gairn-uh . . .]

tell: could you tell me where . . . ? könnten Sie mir sagen, wo . . . ? [kurrn-ten zee meer zah-ghen voh]

temperature die Temperatur [–toor]

tennis Tennis; **tennis court** der Tennisplatz

tennis racket der Tennisschläger [–shlay-gher]; **tennis ball** der Tennisball

tent das Zelt [tselt]

terminal die Endstation [ent-shtats-ee-ohn]

terrible schrecklich [shrecklish]

terrific sagenhaft [zah-ghen-haft]

than als [alts]; **bigger/older than...** größer/älter als... [grurrser/elter...]

thanks, thank you danke(schön) [dank-uh(shurrn)]

    thank you very much vielen Dank [feelen...]

    thank you for your help vielen Dank für Ihre Hilfe [...foor eer-uh hilf-uh]

    YOU MAY THEN HEAR...

    bitteschön, bitte sehr *you're welcome*

that dieser, diese, dieses [deez-er, deez-uh, deez-es]

    that man/that table der Mann (dort)/der Tisch (dort)

    I'd like that one ich möchte das da [ish murrsh-tuh...]

    how do you say that? wie spricht man das aus? [vee shprisht man dass ōwss]

    I think that... ich glaube, daß... [ish glōw-buh dass]

the der, die, das; *(plural)* die

theater das Theater [tay-ah-ter]

their ihr [eer]; **it's their bag/it's theirs** das ist ihre Tasche/das ist ihre [...eer-uh...]

them sie [zee]

    with them mit ihnen [...een-en]

then dann

there dort

    how do I get there? wie komme ich dahin? [vee komm-uh ish dah-hin]

    is there/are there? gibt es? [gheept ess]

    there is/there are es gibt

    there you are *(giving something)* hier, bitte! [heer bittuh]

thermos die Thermosflasche [tairmos-flash-uh]

these diese [deez-uh]

they sie [zee]; **they are** sie sind [zee zinnt]

thick dick

thief der Dieb [deep]

thigh der Schenkel [sh—]

thin dünn [dōnn]

thing das Ding

  I've lost all my things ich habe all meine Sachen verloren [ish hah-buh al mine-uh zah-ken fair-lor-ren]

think denken

  I'll think it over ich werde es mir überlegen [ish vair-duh ess meer ōber-lay-ghen]

  I think so/I don't think so ich denke schon/ich denke nicht [ish denk-uh shohn . . .]

third (adjective) dritte [drit-uh]

thirsty: I'm thirsty ich habe Durst [ish hah-buh dōorst]

this dieser, diese, dieses [deez-er, deez-uh, deez-es]

  can I have this one? kann ich das haben? [. . . dass hah-ben]

  this is my wife/this is Mr. . . . (das ist) meine Frau/(das ist) Herr . . . [mine-uh frōw . . .]

  is this . . . ? ist das . . . ?

those diese (da) [deez-uh (dah)]

  those people diese Leute (da) [. . . loy-tuh . . .]

thread (noun) der Faden [fah-den]

three drei [dry]

throat der Hals [halz]

throttle (motorbike, boat) der Gashebel [gahss-hay-bel]

through durch [dōorsh]

throw (verb) werfen [vair-fen]

thumb der Daumen [dōw-men]

thumbtack die Reißzwecke [rice-tsvecker]

thunder (noun) der Donner

  thunderstorm ein Gewitter [gheh-vitter]

Thursday Donnerstag [donners-tahg]

ticket (train) die Fahrkarte [−kar-tuh]

  (bus) der Fahrschein [−shine]

  (plane) das Ticket

  (cinema) die Eintrittskarte [ine-trits-kar-tuh]

  (cloakroom) die Garderobenmarke [gar-duh-roh-ben-mark-uh]

  (office) die Kasse [kassuh]

» *TRAVEL TIP: see* **bus**

tie *(necktie)* die Krawatte [krav-at-uh]

Tiefgarage *underground parking*

tight *(clothes)* eng

   they're too tight sie sind zu eng [zee zinnt
tsoo . . .]

tights die Strumpfhose [shtrompf-hoh-zuh]

time die Zeit [tsite]

   what's the time? wie spät ist es? [vee shpayt
isst ess]

   I haven't got time ich habe keine Zeit [ish
hah-buh kine-uh . . .]

   for the time being vorläufig [for-loy-fik]

   this time/last time/next time dieses
Mal/letztes Mal/nächstes Mal [deez-es
mahl . . .]

   3 times dreimal [dry-mahl]

   have a good time! viel Vergnügen! [feel
fair-guh-nō̄-ghen]

   timetable *(travel)* der Fahrplan [−plahn]

» *TRAVEL TIP: how to tell the time*

   it's one o'clock es ist ein Uhr [. . . ine oor]

   it's 2/3/4/5/6 o'clock es ist zwei/drei/vier/fünf/
sechs Uhr [tsvy/dry/feer/fōōnf/zex oor]

   it's 5/10/20/25 past 7 est ist fünf/zehn/zwanzig/
fünfundzwanzig (Minuten) nach sieben
[fōōnf/tsayn/tsvan-tsik/fōōnf-ont-tsvan-tsik nahk
zeeben]

   it's quarter past 8/8:15 es ist Viertel nach
acht/acht Uhr fünfzehn [feertel nahk ahkt/ahkt
oor fōōnf-tsayn]

   it's half past 9/9:30 es ist halb zehn/neun Uhr
dreißig [halp tsayn/noyn oor dry-sik]

   it's 25/20 to ten es ist fünf/zehn nach halb
zehn [fōōnf-tsayn nahk halp tsayn]

   it's quarter to eleven es ist Viertel vor elf
[feertel for elf]

   it's 10/5 to eleven es ist zehn/fünf (Minuten)
vor elf [tsayn/fōōnf for elf]

   it's twelve o'clock es ist zwölf (Uhr) [tsvurrlf]

   at . . . um . . . [oom]

» *TRAVEL TIP: notice that in German half past*
nine etc. is said as "half ten".
tip *(noun)* das Trinkgeld [–gelt]
  is the tip included? ist das inklusive
  Bedienung? [isst dass in-kloo-*zee*-vuh
  buh-d*ee*-nȯong]
» *TRAVEL TIP: tip same people as in US; also*
customary to tip in bars
tire der Reifen [ry-fen]
  I need a new tire ich brauche einen neuen
  Reifen [ish brōw*k*-uh ine-en noy-en . . .]
» *TRAVEL TIP: tire pressures*

lb/sq in	18	20	22	24	26	28	30
kg/sq cm	1.3	1.4	1.5	1.7	1.8	2.0	2.1

tired müde [mōō-duh]
  I'm tired ich bin müde [ish . . .]
tissues Papiertaschentücher
  [pa-p*ee*r-tashen-tōō*k*-er]
to: to England nach England [nah*k* . . .]
toast der Toast
tobacco der T*a*bak
tobacconist's der Tabakwarenladen
  [–vah-ren-lah-den]
today heute [hoy-tuh]
toe die Zehe [tsay-uh]
together zusammen [tsoo-zammen]
  we're together wir sind zusammen
  can we pay all together? können wir alles
  zusammen bezahlen? [kurrn-en veer al-less . . .
  buh-tsah-len]
toilet die Toilette [twa-lettuh]
  where are the toilets? wo sind die Toiletten?
  [voh zinnt dee . . .]
  I have to go to the toilet ich muß auf die
  Toilette [ish mȯoss ōwf dee . . .]
  there's no toilet paper es ist kein
  Toilettenpapier da [. . . kine –pa-p*ee*r dah]
  ladies' restroom die Damentoilette
  [dah-men-twa-lettuh]
  men's restroom die Herrentoilette

public restroom öffentliche Toilette
[urrfent-lish-uh twa-lettuh]
» TRAVEL TIP: *there are not very many public*
conveniences in Germany; try the railway
station
tomato die Tomate [tomah-tuh]
  tomato juice der Tomatensaft [−zaft]
tomorrow morgen [mor-ghen]
  tomorrow morning/tomorrow afternoon/
  tomorrow evening morgen früh/morgen
  nachmittag/morgen abend [. . . frōō]
  the day after tomorrow übermorgen
  [ōober−]
  see you tomorrow bis morgen
ton die Tonne [tonn-uh]
» TRAVEL TIP: *1 ton = 1,016 kilos*
1 tonne = 1,000 kilos = metric ton
tongue die Zunge [tsoong-uh]
tonic(water) das Tonic(wasser)
tonight heute abend [hoy-tuh ah-bent]
tonsillitis die Mandelentzündung
  [−ent-tsōōn-doong]
tonsils die Mandeln
too zu [tsoo] *(also)* auch [ōwk]
  that's too much das ist zuviel [dass isst
  tsoo-feel]
tool das Werkzeug [vairk-tsoyg]
tooth der Zahn [tsahn]
  I've got toothache ich habe Zahnweh [ish
  hah-buh −vay]
  toothbrush die Zahnbürste [−bōōrst-uh]
  toothpaste die Zahnpasta
top: on top of . . . auf [ōwf]
  on the top floor im obersten Stock
  at the top oben
total *(noun)* die Endsumme [ent-zoom-uh]
tough *(meat)* zäh [tsay]
tour *(of area)* eine Rundreise [roont-ry-zuh]
  (of town) ein Rundfahrt
  (of castle) ein Rundgang

we'd like to go on a tour of... wir möchten gern eine Reise/eine Rundfahrt/einen Rundgang durch... machen [veer murrsh-ten gairn...]

tourist der Tourist; **I'm only a tourist** ich bin fremd hier [ish bin fremmt heer]
  tourist office das Fremdenverkehrsbüro [frem-den-fair-kairs-bōō-roh]

tow *(verb)* abschleppen [*a*pp-shleppen]
  can you give me a tow? könnten Sie mich abschleppen? [kurrn-ten zee mish...]
  towrope das Abschleppseil [−zile]

towards gegen [g*a*y-ghen]
  he was coming straight towards me er kam geradewegs auf mich zu [air kahm gheh-rah-duh-veggs ōwf mish tsoo]

towel das Handtuch [hant-too*k*]

town die Stadt [shtat]; **in town** in der Stadt
  would you take me into town? würden Sie mich in die Stadt bringen? [vōōrden zee...]

traditional traditionell [tradi-tsee-oh-n*e*l]
  a traditional German meal ein echt deutsches Essen [ine esht doytshes...]

traffic der Verkehr [fair-k*a*ir]
  traffic lights die Ampel

train der Zug [tsoog]
  by train per Bahn [pair...]
  » *TRAVEL TIP: efficient and punctual; if you travel Intercity buy your "Zuschlag"* [tsoo-shlahg] *(surcharge ticket) first*
  YOU MAY HEAR...
  noch jemand zugestiegen? *any more tickets, please?*

tranquilizers Beruhigungsmittel [buh-roo-ig∞ngs−]

translate übersetzen [∞ber-z*e*t-sen]
  would you translate that for me? würden Sie das für mich übersetzen? [vōōrden zee dass fōōr mish...]

transmission *(of car)* das Getriebe [gheh-tr*ee*-buh]

travel: we're traveling around wir reisen
herum [veer ry-zen hair-ꝏm]
travel agent das Reisebüro [ry-zuh-bꝏ-roh]
traveler's check der Travellerscheck
tree der Baum [bōwm]
tremendous enorm [ay-norm]
trip *(noun)* die Reise [ry-zuh]
  (outing) der Ausflug [ōwss-floog]
  have a good trip! gute Reise! [goot-uh . . .]
  we want to go on a trip to . . . wir möchten
  nach . . . fahren [veer murrsh-ten nahk . . .]
trouble die Schwierigkeiten [shvee-rik-kite-en]
  I'm having trouble with . . . ich habe
  Schwierigkeiten mit . . . [ish hah-buh . . .]
trousers die Hose [hoh-zuh]
truck der Last(kraft)wagen der LKW
  [lasst(krafft)vah-ghen, el-kah-vay]
true wahr [vahr]; **it's not true** das ist nicht
  wahr [dass isst nisht . . .]
trunk *(car)* der Kofferraum [−rōwm]
trunks *(swimming)* die Badehose
  [bah-duh-hoh-zuh]
trust: I trust you ich vertraue Ihnen [ish
  fair-trōw-uh een-en]
try *(verb)* versuchen [fair-zꝏk-en]
  can I try it on? kann ich es anprobieren?
  [kan ish ess an-proh-bee-ren]
  can I try? kann ich es versuchen? [kann ish
  ess fair-zꝏ-ken]
T-shirt das T-shirt
Tuesday Dienstag [deenz-tahg]
tunnel der Tunnel
turn: where do we turn off? wo beigen wir ab?
  [voh bee-ghen veer app]
  he turned without indicating er bog ab,
  ohne Zeichen zu geben [air bohg app oh-nuh
  tsy-shen tsoo gay-ben]
twice zweimal [tsvy-mal]
  twice as much doppelt soviel [. . . zoh-feel]
twin beds zwei (Einzel)betten [tsvy (ine-tsel)−]
two zwei [tsvy]

typewriter die Schreibmaschine
[shripe-mash-ee-nuh]
typical typisch [tōō-pish]
U-Bahn subway
ugly häßlich [hess-lish]
ulcer das Geschwür [gheh-shvōōr]
umbrella der Schirm [sheerm]
Umleitung diversion
uncle: my uncle mein Onkel
uncomfortable unbequem [oon-buh-kvaym]
unconscious bewußtlos [buh-voost-lohs]
under unter [oonter]
underdone *(not cooked)* nicht gar [nisht . . .]
understand: I understand ich verstehe [ish
fair-shtay-uh]
  I don't understand das verstehe ich nicht
  do you understand? verstehen Sie?
  [fair-shtay-en zee]
undo aufmachen [ōwf-mah-ken]
unfriendly unfreundlich [oon-froynt-lish]
unhappy unglücklich [oon-glōōck-lish]
United States die Vereinigten Staaten [dee
fair-ine-ik-ten shtah-ten]
unlock aufschließen [ōwf-shlee-sen]
until bis
  not until Tuesday nicht vor Dienstag [nisht
  for . . .]
unusual ungewöhnlich [oon-gheh-vurrn-lish]
up: up in the mountains oben in den Bergen
  he's not up yet er ist noch nicht auf [air isst
  nok nisht ōwf]
  what's up? was ist los? [vass isst lohs]
upside-down verkehrt herum [fair-kairt
  hair-oom]
upstairs oben
urgent dringend [dring-ent]
us uns [oonts]; **it's us** wir sind's [veer zinnts]
use: can I use . . . ? kann ich . . . benutzen? [kan
  ish buh-noot-sen]
useful nützlich [nōōts-lish]

usual(ly) gewöhnlich [gheh-v*u*rrn-lish]
  as usual wie gewöhnlich [vee...]
U-turn die Wende [ven-duh]
vacancy ein (freies) Zimmer
  do you have any vacancies? haben Sie noch
  Zimmer frei? [h*a*h-ben zee no*k* tsimmer fry]
vacate *(room)* räumen [roy-men]
vacation der Urlaub
  I'm on vacation Ich bin im Urlaub/in Ferien
vaccination die Impfung [imp-f*oo*ng]
valid gultig [g*oo*lti*k*]; **how long is it valid
  for?** wie lange gilt es? [vee lang-uh ghilt ess]
valley das Tal [tahl]
valuable wertvoll [vairt-fol]
value *(noun)* der Wert [vairt]
valve das Ventil [ven-t*ee*l]
van der Kombi
  (delivery) der Lieferwagen [l*ee*fer-vah-ghen]
vanilla Vanille [van-*ee*-luh]
varicose veins die Krampfadern [−ah-dern]
veal das Kalbfleisch [kalp-flysh]
vegetables Gemüse [gheh-m*oo*-zuh]
vegetarian *(noun)* ein Vegetarier
  [vay-gheh-t*a*r-ee-er]
ventilator der Ventilator [−l*a*h-tor]
verboten *forbidden*
very sehr [zair]; **very much** sehr
via über [*oo*ber]
video camera die Film Kamera
village das Dorf
vine die Rebe [ray-buh]
vinegar der Essig [−i*k*]
vineyard der Weinberg [v*i*ne-bairk]
vintage der Jahrgang [yahr−]
violent heftig [−i*k*]
visa ein Visum [vee-z*oo*m]
visibility die Sicht [zisht]
visit *(verb)* besuchen [buh-zoo*k*-en]
vodka der Wodka [v−]
voice die Stimme [shtim-uh]

voltage die Spannung [shpan-ⲟong]
Vorsicht! caution
Vorsicht, bißiger Hund beware of the dog
waist die Taille [tal-yuh]
» TRAVEL TIP: waist measurements

US	24	26	28	30	32	34	36	38
Germany	61	66	71	76	80	87	91	97

wait: will we have to wait long? müssen wir lange warten? [mⲟossen veer lang-uh varten]
  wait for me warten Sie auf mich [. . . zee ⲟwf mish]
  I'm waiting for a friend ich warte auf einen Freund [ish var-tuh ⲟwf . . .]
waiter der Kellner; **waiter!** (Herr) Ober!
waitress die Kellnerin
  waitress! Fräulein! [froy-line]
wake: will you wake me up at 7:30? wecken Sie mich, bitte, um 7:30? [vecken zee mish bittuh ⲟom halp ahkt]
Wales Wales [v–]
walk: can we walk there? können wir zu Fuß hingehen? [kurrnen veer tsoo fooss hin-gay-en]
  are there any good walks around here? kann man hier gut wandern? [kan man heer goot vandern]
  walking shoes die Wanderschuhe [–shoo-uh]
wall die Mauer [mⲟwer]
  (inside) die Wand [vannt]
wallet die Brieftasche [breef-tash-uh]
want: I want a . . . ich möchte ein . . . [ish murrsh-tuh]
  I want to talk to . . . ich möchte mit . . . sprechen
  what do you want? was möchten Sie? [vass murrsh-ten zee]
  I don't want to ich will nicht [ish vill nisht]
  he wants to . . . er will . . . [air vill]
  they don't want to sie wollen nicht
warm warm [varm]
warning die Warnung [varn-ⲟong]

Wartesaal *waiting room*

was: I was/he was/it was ich war/er war/es war
[... var]

wash: can you wash these for me? könnten
Sie diese für mich waschen? [kurrnt-en zee
dee-zuh für mish vashen]

where can I wash...? wo kann ich...
waschen? [voh...]

washing machine die Waschmaschine
[vash-mash-een-uh]

washer *(for bolt, etc.)* die Dichtung [dish-tœng]

wasp die Wespe [vesp-uh]

watch: *(wrist-)* die (Armband)uhr
[(armbannt)oor]

will you watch...for me? würden Sie für
mich auf... aufpassen? [vōorden zee für mish
ōwf... ōwf-pas-en]

watch out! Achtung! [ahk-tœng]

water das Wasser [vasser]

can I have some water? kann ich Wasser
haben? [kan ish hah-ben]

hot and cold running water fließend kalt
und warm Wasser [flee-sent...]

waterfall der Wasserfall [−fal]

waterproof wasserdicht [−disht]

waterskiing Wasserskilaufen [−shee-lōwfen]

way: we'd like to eat the German way wir
möchten gerne typisch deutsch essen [veer
murrsh-ten gairn-uh tœpish doytsh essen]

could you tell me the way to...? könnten
Sie mir den Weg nach... sagen? [kurrn-ten zee
meer dayn vayg nahk... zah-ghen] *see* **where**
for answers

we wir [veer]; **we are** wir sind [veer zinnt]

weak schwach [shvahk]

weather das Wetter [v−]

what lousy weather! so ein Hundewetter!
[zoh ine hœn-duh−]

what's the weather forecast? was sagt der
Wetterbericht? [vas zahgt dair −buh-risht]
YOU MAY THEN HEAR...

überwiegend heiter *generally fine*
leichte/schwere Schauer *light/heavy showers*
Gewitter *thundery*
sonnig, warm, kalt *sunny, warm, cold*
Wednesday Mittwoch [mit-vo*k*]
week die Woche [voc*k*-uh]
   a week today/tomorrow heute/morgen in
   einer Woche [hoy-tuh/mor-ghen in ine-er ...]
   at the weekend am Wochenende [am
   voc*k*en-end-uh]
weight das Gewicht [gheh-v*i*sht]
well: I'm not feeling well ich fühle mich nicht
   wohl [ish f*oo*l-uh mish nisht vole]
   he's not well es geht ihm nicht gut [ess gayt
   eem nisht goot]
   how are you? very well, thanks wie geht's?
   danke, gut! [vee gayts dankuh goot]
   you speak English very well Sie sprechen
   sehr gut Englisch [zee spreshen zair goot
   eng-glish]
Welsh walisisch [val-*ee*-zish]
   Welshman/-woman Waliser(in)
were: you were Sie waren [zee varen]
   (familiar) du warst [doo varst]
   you were *(plural)* Sie waren; *(familiar)* ihr
   wart [eer vart] *see* **you**
   we were wir waren [veer ...]
   they were sie waren
west der Westen [v–]
West Indian westindisch [vest-indish]
   (person) Westinder; *(woman)* Westinderin
West Indies die Westindischen Inseln [dee
   vest-indishen inzeln]
wet naß [nass]
what was [vass]
   what is that? was ist das?
   what for? wozu? [voh-tsoo]
   what room? welches Zimmer? [velshes
   tsimmer]
wheel das Rad [raht]
wheelchair der Rollstuhl [rol-shtool]

0	null [nœl]	17	siebzehn [zeep–]
1	eins [ine-ts]	18	achtzehn
2	zwei [tsvy]	19	neunzehn
3	drei [dry]	20	zwanzig
4	vier [feer]		[tsvan-tsik]
5	fünf [fœnf]	21	einundzwangzig
6	sechs [zex]		[ine-œnt–]
7	sieben [zeeben]	22	zweiundzwanzig
8	acht [ahkt]	23	dreiundzwanzig
9	neun [noyn]	24	vierundzwanzig
10	zehn [tsayn]	25	fünfundzwanzig
11	elf	26	sechsundzwanzig
12	zwölf [tsvurrlf]	27	siebenundzwanzig
13	dreizehn	28	achtundzwanzig
	[dry-tsayn]	29	neunundzwanzig
14	vierzehn	30	dreißig [dry-sik]
15	fünfzehn	31	einunddreißig
16	sechzehn		

40	vierzig	70	siebzig [zeep–]
50	fünfzig	80	achtzig
60	sechzig	90	neunzig
100	hundert[hœndert]	101	hunderteins
175	hundertfünfundsiebzig		
	[hœndertfœnf-zeep-tsik]		
200	zweihundert		
1,000	tausend [tōw-zent]		
2,000	zweitausend		
1,000,000	eine Million [ine-uh mil-ee-yone]		

NB: the German comma is a decimal point; for thousands use a period, e.g. 2.000

The German alphabet

a [ah] **b** [bay] **c** [tsay] **d** [day] **e** [ay] **f** [eff]
g [gay] **h** [hah] **i** [ee] **j** [yot] **k** [kah] **l** [el]
m [em] **n** [en] **o** [oh] **p** [pay] **q** [koo] **r** [air]
s [ess] **t** [tay] **u** [oo] **v** [fōw] **w** [vay] **x** [eeks]
y [ōōp-zee-lon] **z** [tset] **ß** = ss